HELEN G
and the sp

throughout her memoirs. From early steps in education attending a Steiner nursery school through to the rigid formality and structure of multi-academy trusts where she worked as a director, Helen often found herself pushing up against authority.

Being a teacher was absolutely not in the plan, and yet thirty years spent in education saw Helen move from a classroom teacher to two very successful headships and three director posts. Leadership during the pandemic brought new and unexpected challenges and the need for a change.

Helen is married with two grown up daughters, three grown up step children and lives back in Gloucestershire where she was brought up. Following her retirement in 2021, she now volunteers at a hedgehog rescue centre, is a trained appropriate adult, reads avidly and tries to tire out her beloved spaniels, Frida and Fern.

An Accidental Headship

HELEN GLASS

SilverWood

Published in 2022 by SilverWood Books

SilverWood Books Ltd
14 Small Street, Bristol, BS1 1DE, United Kingdom
www.silverwoodbooks.co.uk

ISBN 978-1-80042-216-2 (paperback)

British Library Cataloguing in Publication Data
A CIP catalogue record for this book is
available from the British Library

Page design and typesetting by SilverWood Books

For my daughters, Dina and Leah, who travelled much of this journey with me.

A marble in the eye

"Where are we going, John?" I'd asked my dad over and over on the bus into town.

"You're going to school, Boo."

Strangers on the bus must have been perplexed by this exchange as we looked like father and daughter, yet I called him John. The simple truth was that I called my dad by his first name until I went to primary school. I'm not sure why or how that started, as I called my mum "Mummy" and never Maggie. But, then, there were several unusual features about my upbringing. Mum was the breadwinner and taught at a secondary school in Stroud. Dad stayed at home with me when mum returned to work after maternity leave and until I went to primary school. Later down the line, he took up a teaching post. I didn't appreciate how unusual that was until I went to proper school and it became apparent that nobody else's dad stayed at home with them and most of my friends' mums didn't work. You don't need to be trained in Jungian psychology to work out that this upbringing probably had some impact. In very simple terms, as far as I knew, mums worked and brought home interesting books, food and tales of the day and dads played, cooked, and did interesting stuff with clay and pencils. As a parent, I now understand how extremely hard this role reversal was for both of them and, no matter how trendy and groundbreaking, mum must have been torn every day between her professional self and wanting to be a mum, and dad was often very isolated as the only man at the toddler group and at the nursery gates.

When we finally arrived at our destination, the world of formal education opened its doors to me. I say formal, but my early and formative education did not take place in a conventional setting. My parents enrolled me at a Steiner nursery and, although I was only little and my memories are rather hazy, I remember one particular incident very clearly indeed!

Hands up if you know what eurythmy' is? That is a sort of a joke, by the way, because, from what I remember of eurythmy sessions, it involved a fair bit of running around the wooden-floored hallway while waving hands and arms in the air 'like the wind blowing through the trees'. Eurythmy, a practice developed by Rudolf Steiner, an Austrian philosopher, is described as an 'expressive movement art' and it was claimed to have therapeutic qualities. This was all rather lost on me at aged three and my peers and I just knew it represented fun and the chance to throw ourselves around pretending to be animals and elements of nature.

Our eurythmy teacher was Miss Blathwaite. She was both kindly and formidable. Each week, she arrived for our sessions, and I can remember her as physically substantial with grey hair in a bun. We hopped and spun around gleefully in our pants and vests with not a shred of self-consciousness. That is one of the wonderful things about being three. On this particular day, we had been playing an intricate game involving marbles, wooden bridges and makeshift tunnels. We rolled marbles that glinted back at us like eyeballs and shrieked with excitement each time one emerged from a cardboard tube tunnel or made its rolling, wobbly way along a bridge. As with all good things, we quickly grew bored and were keen to explore what else we could do with marbles. Would they bounce? This was a question of physics that we were keen to explore. Imagine our joy when we discovered that if you threw one down hard enough on the floor, it would indeed bounce right back up. We set to this challenge with gusto. Even at that tender age, I was someone who would take a situation and push it a little bit further than perhaps was wise. I took a marble and threw it harder than was necessary. I watched it bounce and arc impressively. Time slowed and, with something akin to fascination mixed with horror, I watched as the marble's onward journey set it on a direct collision course with Miss Blathwaite. Worse than that, much worse. It collided with her eye and the cry that went up was truly blood-curdling. Everyone stopped what they were doing and looked first at Miss Blathwaite and then at me. This was not good. I was in big trouble. I was still holding marbles in my other hand.

"Helen, come here."

I shuffled across the hall towards our teacher and Miss Blathwaite.

"Helen, why did you throw the marble at Miss Blathwaite?"

"I was playing," I replied.

"But Miss Blathwaite could have been blinded."

"I was only playing."

I don't remember what happened after that, but I know the marbles were packed away, Miss Blathwaite went for a long sit down with something cooling over her eye and I knew I had done something unbelievably bad. I got the distinct impression that my reputation was damaged beyond repair but, aged three, I had no idea what to do about it.

In Miss Cherry's garden

When I wasn't terrorising staff at my nursery school, I was with my dad. We went for long walks through the local woods and on the nearby common, collecting interesting stones and feathers or picking cobnuts, rosehips, blackberries and puffballs, depending on the season. We were accompanied on our walks by Pye, our Welsh Border collie cross. She always found something smelly and revolting to roll in. We would hose her down when we got home, but she would invariably roll in the garden and get mucky all over again.

As a small child, my world was never dull and I have flashes of memory from that time, involving lunchtime programmes such as *Mary, Mungo and Midge*, *Pogles' Wood* and *Mr Benn*. I loved them all, but *Mr Benn* was my favourite because each episode was different apart from the familiar saying, "As if by magic, the shopkeeper appeared." All young children enjoy repetition and recognising what is coming and I liked saying that phrase out loud. But what I really liked was that Mr Benn could be someone entirely new and different for the duration of each episode and he always left with a small souvenir of his adventure which anchored the fictional past journey in the factual present.

I spent a lot of time in the company of the various elderly ladies in the village to whom my dad gave art classes. I wandered through lovely gardens, met pampered dogs, and was spoiled with little gifts from many of these ladies. I liked them and they liked me. It was a good arrangement all round.

The local post office was run by Miss Cherry. I have a vague memory of her face as she peered at me from behind the counter when we popped in for stamps. What I loved about the post office was the display of Matchbox cars that held a prominent position at the front of the counter. I ran my fingers longingly over the clear Perspex covers that protected the cars from small and inquisitive fingers. Sometimes mum or dad would buy one for me and that was a real treat.

Miss Cherry was one of those people who did not really know how to talk to children. She tried, in her own way, but I felt instinctively that she didn't like me and, so, I was wary of her. She always tried her best to make conversation, but things never sounded warm or genuine and, even as a little girl, I could feel that. On one notable occasion, dad and I went to the post office and, as was always the case, dad stopped to have a little conversation with Miss Cherry.

She looked over the counter at me and, in a voice that was meant to be friendly but didn't quite work, said, "What a little flower you are."

Quick as a flash and with no shadow of doubt, I piped up, "If I was a flower, I wouldn't want to grow in your garden."

Dad told me this story many times as I was growing up. He said he had to get out of the post office as quickly as he could, because he could hardly contain his laughter and didn't want to add insult to injury.

When trolls were good

I graduated from life at nursery school and was ready for the real thing. My parents enrolled me in the village primary school. By the time I got to school I already knew how to read. Mum was brilliant at sourcing unusual and stimulating books and resources. Not for me the drudgery of the twee middle-classness of Peter and Jane. Certainly, I read them at home and at school, because they were unavoidable in the 1970s but, happily for me, mum bought the *Little Nippers* and *Nippers* books that featured diverse families predominantly from working-class backgrounds. I loved those books and I have them to this very day. *Tracy's Story*, a tale about false eyelashes and a caterpillar, was pure gold and so much more engaging than Peter and Jane and their wretched dog, Pat, who never did anything interesting.

You would think that being able to read already would have been a good thing. It wasn't. I was regarded as a bit of a nuisance in that regard as I would say quite loudly and quite often, "I've already read that one, Miss." Differentiation by input was not exactly the fashion back then and what the teacher really wanted was for everyone to do pretty much the same thing at the same time, because that was much easier to manage. Aged nearly five, I was not deliberately trying to be difficult, precocious, or a show-off; I simply didn't understand why

I was expected to learn something I already knew. I was certainly not the only one to experience this and many of you probably recall similar frustrations.

The school headmistress, Miss Trowbridge, had a rather unorthodox approach to many things. She was of her generation and her beliefs were somewhat at odds with the newfangled ways of the 1970s. But she cared not a jot and the world of the school was all the world that we knew. She was generally kind, but had a ferocious streak and could be very scary indeed as I discovered in my first year in Infants.

Back then, school lunches were proper meals, eaten sitting down at tables with real cutlery and crockery. Not for us those drooping slices of pizza followed by a muffin and washed down with fizzy, fruit-flavoured water. We even had appropriate condiments to go with each dish – mint sauce for our roast lamb, apple sauce for pork, and so forth. Although the food was excellent, there were, of course, things that I did not like and, occasionally, the cook had an off day but, in the main, we were well fed and we thoroughly enjoyed our lunches.

I had not encountered steak and kidney pudding before attending school and I was not at all sure about either the name or the look of it. The kidney looked the wrong side of grey in colour, and the suet pastry topping was heavy and stuck to the roof of my mouth. I gave up after two mouthfuls and tried to squeeze the rest of the pudding into the smallest pile I could at the edge of my plate. I ate the vegetables and gravy and then admitted defeat. Our plates were cleared away and that was the end of the matter. Or so I thought.

Morning assemblies were a jolly occasion. We infants were not considered responsible enough for hymn books, but we were very much encouraged to join in with the hymn singing, which led to some interesting interpretations of the lyrics. Our favourite hymn was "Onward Christian Soldiers" and we sang this as loudly as our little five-year-old lungs would allow. On this particular morning, Miss Trowbridge read a Bible story, we sang a couple more hymns and, as there were no birthdays to celebrate that morning, we expected to file back to our classrooms. But Miss Trowbridge paused dramatically and fixed us with a very serious glare.

"Boys and girls," she said, "I am very sad and disappointed to tell you that somebody from our school has been wasting food. There are starving children in the world but somebody from our school did not eat their lunch yesterday. Mrs Gregory, please bring it in."

Mrs Gregory ran the kitchen and was also Miss Trowbridge's sister, a fact that, for some reason, fascinated us.

To our collective astonishment, Mrs Gregory disappeared and then reappeared with a plate containing the now slightly congealed, and even less appetising, steak and kidney pudding that I had rejected. I could feel my cheeks burning and tears prickle in my eyes. Miss Trowbridge took the offending plate from her sister and held it aloft like John the Baptist's head.

"Who left this perfectly good food? I want whoever did this to own up."

Her demand was met with stony silence. Amid much coughing and shuffling, I was poked in the back from the child sitting behind me. I would not own up. I would not do the walk of shame. I would never be able to look at a steak and kidney pie again.

This was an isolated incident and my memories of Miss Trowbridge are, in the main, very positive indeed. She told fabulous stories during assembly, encouraged us to sing our hearts out and had a real-life family of Trolls. Or so we believed. Trolls and trolling mean something very different today to what they meant for us in our village primary school. Miss Trowbridge's Trolls were legendary, and we loved those special days when one of them made an appearance. They came at Easter, Christmas, for staff birthdays, at the end of term and, sometimes, just for the sheer hell of it. Miss Trowbridge would receive the secret message that a Troll had arrived. We were then led out of the assembly hall to find the Troll and see what it had left. This usually involved chocolate or sweets and, on one particularly exciting day, a chocolate tool for each of us. We delighted over our chocolate hammers, spanners and pliers. I think Miss Trowbridge was onto something with all those Trolls, as a quick internet search suggests that vintage Trolls from the 1960s and 1970s go for a surprising amount of money these days. Now I wish I'd hung onto mine!

A bit of God bother

My primary school was a church school, and this came with many obligations. We were marched down to the church for hymn practice and each week the vicar came to us to deliver a sermon. These were delivered in a booming monotone, invariably sin-focused and utterly dull. Now the Old Testament contains some cracking stories and it wouldn't have taken much to choose a lively story to tell us. But the vicar always went for the driest and most shock-free tale possible. We infants did not like him at all, mostly because he ignored us and projected his gaze and voice over our heads to the juniors seated cross-legged at the back of the hall. But things didn't improve when we became juniors and, finally, something had to give.

There were two sisters from the same family in my class. I'll call them Donna and Karen. They were from a hard-up family with seven children – three boys and four girls – who, at that time, ranged in age from one year to eleven years old. The youngest child was a source of great fascination. The children were all quite grubby and smelly, and often had nits. Looking back, the family was clearly struggling and schools in those days could be quite heartless places. Children can be cruel and teachers even more so. This is a sad and shameful truth about schools that I came to understand quite early on, and it is something that informed my practice as a teacher and head teacher. There is a world of difference between being firm and being hard.

Each day, the mum would wheel the baby of the family to the school in his pushchair. Invariably, he sucked with gusto on a baby's bottle that contained what looked suspiciously like Camp coffee. Some of you will be old enough to remember that particular elixir of delight. My mum gave it to me too, but not when I was a baby and not from a feeding bottle. If the health visitor ever commented on this, it clearly had no impact, and the baby grew up to be a strapping chap so, clearly, he was none the worse for the Camp coffee.

I digress, but bear with me, because to understand the significance of what came to pass with the vicar, a bit of context is required. It was Friday morning and Bible story day. We settled in for a boring time and were not disappointed. The vicar's voice droned on, not unlike the teacher in the Peanuts cartoons. We soon stopped listening. Karen was making a good show of listening, but Donna had totally given up. Neither sister could read, so it was insensitive, to put it mildly, of the vicar to ask them to "follow the story" in the book. I was in half a mind to point out to the vicar that neither of my classmates could read and maybe he might go a bit more slowly or something. But I thought better of it and calculated that things might not go well if I were to open my mouth. On and on he went. We fidgeted, tipping on our chairs, wobbling our pencil Gonks so that their arms and legs shimmied and did a host of other tricks to make the time go faster. All of this had an impact, and the vicar became redder and redder in the face as he realised that he had well and truly lost our attention. Reader, he never had it in the first place. This made him incredibly angry and disinclined to 'suffer the little children'. He started to bellow at us, randomly but viciously. He decided to home in on poor Donna.

"Donna," he roared, "you haven't been listening or following in your book, so I am going to ask you a question and perhaps you'll pay more attention next time. What was the name of the disciple in the story?"

Donna flushed and looked at her desk. She mumbled, "I dunno."

We all knew that the vicar knew that Donna and Karen couldn't read, so what he did next was calculated and cruel.

"I think you mean 'I don't know'. Speak properly, for goodness' sake. Right, if you can't remember, you had better read the passage back to the whole class and then perhaps you'll stop wasting everyone's time."

There are moments in life when you gain a new understanding of the world and once you have it, you can never quite go back. Donna sat in silence. The vicar kept pressing her to read. He tried to encourage us to turn against her by mocking her, but we too sat silent. This horrible game of David and Goliath went on for several painful minutes but then, just as in the Bible story, David turned.

Donna looked up, her eyes full of tears which she wiped away angrily. "You're a bloody bastard!" she yelled at the top of her voice, as she noisily shoved her chair backwards and fled the room.

We waited, hardly daring to breathe. This was truly terrible. Surely the world would end, well Donna's world at any rate. The vicar looked bewildered. Somehow, he seemed smaller. Goliath had fallen.

The vicar went in search of Donna and found her with her face pressed into the railings by the front playground. We watched from the classroom window, craning to see what would happen. The vicar bent down to be at her height and spoke quietly to her. She took his hand and he brought her back into the classroom. We rushed back to our seats like a frantic tide returning to shore. But we need not have worried. The vicar was subdued and thoughtful for the rest of the lesson, Donna seemed ok, and nothing further was said, but we all knew something that we hadn't known before – grown-ups could be toppled.

Angry Arrow

All good things must come to an end and so it was with Miss Trowbridge and her Trolls. The former retired and the latter left with her, never to return. In her place was a new head teacher, Mr Frape. He was very charismatic, very Welsh, and definitely not into Trolls. He also read fabulous stories to us in assembly, was keen on music of all sorts and had ambitions for a summer fête that turned out to be a mixed blessing.

The day of the fête dawned. The sky was blue, and the sun was high in the sky. A perfect day for a fête. I was very excited as I'd been selected as one of the squaws to accompany Mr Frape's procession. Mr Frape was to be Chief Angry Arrow. I must apologise for the total lack of political correctness. Why this theme was chosen is anyone's guess, but I suspect it had a lot to do with making an entrance and that was something Mr Frape was keen to do.

To maximise the authenticity of his grand entrance as Chief Angry Arrow, Mr Frape had borrowed a horse from the local riding stables to be his steed as he rode triumphantly onto the village green in front of the school. We were waiting in eager anticipation when we saw, from a distance, Mr Frape, aka Angry Arrow, plodding towards us on a docile-looking horse being led along by one of the stablehands. Mr Frape was resplendent in his outfit and full warpaint to further enhance the look.

He appeared to be enjoying himself immensely and was getting into his stride very nicely. The horse proceeded at a steady pace until it reached the railings in front of the school where it was due to be tethered. Now, whether it was a blast from the loudspeaker announcing where to buy tombola tickets, a passing wasp or just bad luck, suddenly the tranquil scene erupted. The horse gave a panicked whinny, reared up on its hind legs, pulled free from the stablehand and, most shockingly of all, dislodged Angry Arrow.

To say Angry Arrow was not expecting to be unceremoniously chucked would be an understatement. The onlooking crowd of parents, pupils and assorted village folk didn't know whether to laugh or cry. Well, that is not strictly true. Out of the corner of my eye I caught sight of my mum who was almost crying with laughter. Angry Arrow was definitely not laughing, in fact he wasn't even smiling.

Those who can

Teaching was absolutely the last thing I wanted to do, and I was confident that I would never go down that route, ever! I remember my parents' piles of marking and the hours they spent preparing lessons. Mum would have a PVC bag next to her chair full to the brim with exercise books or folders of written assignments. I enjoyed helping her to sort her reports into piles and counting the votes for the annual election of Form Captain and Vice Form Captain. The neat rows of red ticks or noughts for attendance or absence in mum's register were always a source of fascination and I used to create my own fantasy classes and register them, very strictly! I remember dad's art coursework spread all over the living room floor and how he would swing between frustration and elation as each piece of work was considered and assessed on its various merits. Staffroom banter and close and enduring friendships were a clear attraction for both mum and dad and, over the years, many of their colleagues and colleagues' children and later grandchildren became as familiar to me as members of my own family. Yet, despite the obvious draws of the teaching profession, there was something about the routines and the compliance required that made me shudder. It was not for me. No thank you very much!

My grandfather, great uncle and, indeed, several relatives on my

Welsh side of the family had been teachers, so you might say it was in the blood. But I was confident that something more exciting lay ahead for me. The trouble was that I didn't know what that was and, following a robust letter from my maternal grandfather telling me it was high time I started to earn a living, I panicked and signed up for a PGCE at King's College, London.

In September 1989, I embarked on what would turn out to be the first steps along a career path that would wind into the future for the next thirty years or more. I honestly thought I would do the course, get the teaching practice under my belt, and then start my proper career. Who was I kidding! To say I loved teaching at that stage would not be truthful. To say that I found my vocation would also be stretching things. What was evident was that I had fallen into a world that often surprised me and charmed me, but which also frustrated me and made me despair. They sometimes say that those who rebelled at school themselves make good teachers because they can empathise more with disaffected teens. I think there is some truth in that, and the poacher turned gamekeeper was a pretty accurate analogy in my case.

Gloucestershire grammar

I was brought up in Amberley and was unaware of the arch rivalry between valley and hill. But, when I started secondary school, I soon discovered that those of us brought up in the villages on the hills above Stroud were seen as posh and were given the cold shoulder by the valley kids. This social hierarchy was no doubt an historical throwback but, historical or not, it was a problem that had to be overcome. I railed against being called 'posh' because it upset my socialist sensibility. It was an early taste of the class system and it tasted bitter to me. My friends at primary school had come from all sorts of backgrounds and I liked them equally. It wasn't that I didn't understand the advantages that some children had, including ponies, swimming pools and every type of Sindy doll ever produced, or that I didn't notice that some friends wore clothes handed down from their big brothers or sisters and sometimes were a bit pongy. Those things simply didn't interest me as much as what they were like to play with at playtime and how much fun they were. I assumed this egalitarian view was shared. I was wrong.

I remember winding down the road into Stroud from the common where the bus picked us up. We were a tad conspicuous in our pink and white striped blouses, grey blazers with pink piping and bright pink ties. The boys at the grammar school got off more lightly in a more ordinary school uniform and didn't stand out the way the girls did. I remember the tightness of my Clarks Cordelia shoes rubbing on my ankles and the weight of the leather satchel that was almost as big as me. I must have looked an absolute sight, and the look was topped off by huge brown framed glasses. Not to put too fine a point on it, but I looked like Stamp Bug, which you may remember from the 1980s. It was not a good look.

Our tutor base was a terrapin hut with a linoleum floor. The heater was covered by a metal cage that had multiple indentations in the top created by the bottoms of numerous girls trying to keep warm. I know because I became one of those girls and added my own indentations. For the whole of the first year, we sat in alphabetical order and that was where the fun began.

The two girls directly in front of me were from the valley and once they found out that I was from Amberley, they both turned around in their seats, looked me up and down and said, in unison, "You're posh then, aren't you."

This was a rhetorical question, apparently, but I felt my socialist credentials bristling. Mustering my best non-posh voice, I said, without a hint of irony, "I ain't posh." This came out as an embarrassing squawk, made me sound utterly ridiculous and only made matters worse.

The two girls snorted with laughter, flicked their hair in utter contempt and pretty much ignored me after that.

Come up to the lab

In secondary education over the years, it has, now and again, been the fashion to keep Year Seven students in a bubble and separate from the rest of the school. It has been argued that the transition from primary to secondary school is difficult and should be a more gradual process. Sometimes it is suggested that creating a staff team with specialist knowledge of Year Sevens and their foibles is beneficial. While I can see the rationale, I disagree with these arguments and, if anyone had suggested keeping us away from the rest of the school population while we matured in our 'pod', I am confident there would have been a mini mutiny. While we were nervous about the older girls, finding our way around the new school and a number of other issues, we wanted to be in the big pond, swimming with the big fish. Those of us from small, village primary schools were particularly excited about having lessons in specialist rooms and areas, about having a real gym with ropes and apparatus, cookery rooms, art studios and science labs. These spaces filled our imaginations and, in the main, did not disappoint.

Science was greatly anticipated and the opportunity to wear lab coats and safety goggles was thrilling. We may have imagined that we looked like proper boffins from *Tomorrow's World* when, in reality, we looked more like the Minions from *Despicable Me*, but we cared not a jot. How many flames of ambition to study medicine, dentistry and the like were fanned in those labs? I was never destined for science in any shape or form and had to reluctantly put aside my childhood dream of becoming a vet. Science and I didn't mix.

In the first few weeks of secondary school, we did a lot of practicals and there was no shortage of opportunities to burn, poison or gas ourselves but, somehow, we survived. Our teachers drilled the safety rules into us. We knew not to bring food into the labs, we understood the difference between a roaring flame and…the other ones, and we knew that picking up tongs that were holding a flask while it heated over a Bunsen burner was not a good idea. I still get a little flutter of adrenaline when I remember rolling globules of mercury in the palm of my hand and lobbing asbestos heat mats into the cupboard at the end of a practical.

We always looked forward to demonstrations of potentially dangerous or risky experiments and gathering around or close to the fume cupboard always signalled something VERY DANGEROUS AND EXCITING! One fine morning, we gathered like proper scientists around said fume cupboard, earnestly pushing our safety specs up our noses to avoid missing anything, while our science teacher mixed chemicals with a glass stirrer. A noxious, amber gas formed that was soon sucked up the vent of the fume cupboard. It was sort of exciting but, when we asked if we could have a go, the teacher said "No" and it became a bit dull. The teacher brought the flask out of the fume cupboard and was about to embark on a tedious lecture about safety when… BANG!…the flask exploded, sending large shards of glass around the lab. One girl was unlucky enough to have a large shard cut her hand, but this was nothing compared to the earth-shattering humiliation of having the science teacher improvise a dressing using an old-fashioned sanitary towel he had to hand. For those of you who are too young or too male to have encountered those old sanitary towels, they were the thickness of a small duvet and had loops at either end to attach to…come to think of it, I have no idea what they were meant to attach to, but the poor girl had to bear the embarrassment of having a sanitary towel wrapped around her hand with one loop around her thumb and the other around her little finger. It was, to be fair, quick thinking on the part of the teacher, but such is the peculiar psychology of pre-teens and teens that my classmate would probably have preferred to have had her hand amputated there and then in the lab than suffer the indignity of wearing a big old sanitary towel around it.

Exploding flasks were just the warm-up and, while I wasn't destined for a career in science, my imagination was fired up from time to time. Bunsen burners held a slightly unhealthy fascination for me and, while I was no pyromaniac, I loved bonfires, fireworks, making toast over an open fire and using a magnifying glass to set fire to stuff. I blame (or, rather, thank) my dad for that because he introduced me to all those delights.

One day, I wondered what would happen if I held my biro in the Bunsen burner flame. If I played with it a little and teased it back and forth across the heat, what then? I was deeply engrossed as I gently rolled my pen and moved it back and forth through the flame. I was fascinated to see it metamorphose from a regular blue biro into a curiously curling, dripping biro. Salvador Dali would have approved of this. Unfortunately, my teacher did not.

"Helen Ayling, what on earth are you doing? Order mark."

An order mark was a terrible thing. It was two steps away from a detention. I was the first person in the class to receive one.

Had I learned my lesson? Well, yes and no. I didn't melt any more pens, but the wonderful thing about science is the endless possibilities to experiment. One of the hard rules drummed into us was that we were not to eat in the lab. This made sense and we appreciated the dormant dangers of chemicals spilled on benches, a smear of mercury and a crumb or 200 of asbestos. However, when you are eleven, an acid drop is an acid drop, and I'm not talking sulfuric acid. One very dull experiment involved dunking acid drop sweets into various liquids, leaving them for an eternity (or so it seemed) and then seeing which liquid caused them to dissolve most quickly. This was so mind-numbingly boring, slow and, frankly, pointless that I am sure you will understand that what followed couldn't really be helped. My lab bench partner and I thought there would be very little harm in sampling the acid drops but, before we knew it, we had consumed our entire allowance. We thought our actions had gone unnoticed, but we thought wrong.

Too late, we heard the rustling of a lab coat, the clip-clop of brogues and the dreaded words, "Order marks! Helen and Rachel, I am issuing you both with order marks for the destruction of scientific equipment!"

We stifled our giggles, shifted the acid drops in our mouths and knew that we were destined for paths other than science.

Three years of secondary school left its mark on me. I didn't quite fit the mould. I was very capable in most subjects, but struggled terribly with maths. And at a grammar school it was expected that you could do everything well. Looking back, I am glad that I had my academic struggles because they undoubtedly informed my approaches as a teacher and my ability to empathise with youngsters who found things hard. I knew the humiliation of being asked to put my work on the board and the withering sarcasm that was the favourite teaching tool of some of my teachers. I remember feeling sick with nerves before some classes, angry and frustrated with myself because maths just wouldn't stick in my head. I used to play up to distract attention from my incompetence and sometimes just to keep my spirits up.

Edith Piaf

There was a certain irony that Mrs Parker, my Year Nine maths teacher, was also my form tutor. She was endlessly patient, both as a teacher and a tutor. She carefully explained concepts to me and to my classmates in the bottom set for maths. We would smile and nod enthusiastically as the penny dropped and a flash of understanding lit up our world. But that understanding never lasted and, at each lesson, the same concepts had to be explained and demonstrated again, only to run through our brains like water through fingers. I don't know if I can explain what this is like for those of you who have always found maths easy or at least within your grasp, but I will try.

Imagine being given the ingredients to make a cake. Each ingredient has been weighed and placed on the table in front of you. You turn away to wash your hands and don your apron. When you turn around, one of the ingredients is missing. You can't remember which one, but you know that where there were five before, now there are only four. You proceed to mix the ingredients you have but in the wrong order because, with one thing missing, the original recipe doesn't really make sense. The result is inedible, bears no resemblance to what the picture looks like in the recipe book but, worse than that, you still can't remember which ingredient is missing because that memory simply didn't stick and, even though you have a recipe in front of you in black and white, somehow you can't cross reference that with what you have in front of you. For me, this memory block was infuriating, humiliating, and confusing because I didn't experience this in any other subject. I wasn't great at science, not because I didn't understand it, but because I found much of it so boring that I tuned out. Even as I write this, I can feel that fuzzy cloud forming in my head, my heart rate increasing, and a slight feeling of queasiness coming over me. So many decades later, the reaction remains strong, and my heart continues to go out to all who struggle with learning. I get it.

If I have any regrets about my school days, it is that I didn't speak up more and explain how maths made me feel and what I needed. But I didn't know what I needed and part of the tragedy for those who experience learning difficulties of any sort is that we so often feel a deep shame and embarrassment. Had I been educated in a gentler regime, perhaps my struggles with maths would have been treated differently. I may have been screened for a specific need. Who knows? My parents did their very best to help me and were aware of my struggles. Mrs Parker was kind and patient, and I didn't dread her classes or experience the eye rolling and contemptuous and angry crosses that other maths teachers issued against my many many wrong answers and there were many, many wrong answers.

My Year Nine tutor base was a bit basic. But we liked it because we were in the last terrapin hut and surrounded by playing fields and open space. As we stepped down the little flight of steps from room 36, as it was called, we were immediately in the fresh air, surrounded by birdsong, with clover and daisies growing underfoot and we could easily cast off the shackles of the classroom and feel free. There, we discussed the top ten featured on *Top of the Pops* the night before, practised dance routines for the fortnightly disco at Minchinhampton youth club, played Top Trumps or just nattered. We always had so much to talk about and breaks and lunchtimes were never long enough to fit it all in, so some overspill was inevitable but risky, as talking in class was dimly viewed and came with the risk of an order mark or, worse still, a detention. We dreaded the thought of both these punishments, although, as someone who had managed to acquire order marks in the first year, by Year Nine, I was a little hardened.

Top of the Pops was hugely important to us, as was the Top 20 countdown on Sunday on Radio 1. I taped the songs I liked and created endless mixtapes. Being a teenager in the late 1970s and early to mid-1980s was fantastic as we moved from punk to the New Romantics and everything in between. This gave us enormous scope for self-expression, and anything went. Our male counterparts at the grammar school were as likely as we were to rock up at parties wearing make-up and we were free to wear the blackest outfits we could find and wear our hair gelled and spiked. I imagine every generation thinks its teen times were the best, but I don't just think it, I know it!

One sunny day, at the end of lunchtime, we spilled back into room 36 for afternoon registration. My friends seemed somehow extra giggly and there was something afoot, but I didn't think much of it. We had been taking delight in mocking a rather absurd song that had made it into the charts in 1979, namely "I'm only a poor little sparrow". I was about to find out why it kept us entertained over lunch.

"Ok, girls, settle down, I need to take the register."

The usual shuffling about ensued, with the unnecessarily loud closing of desk lids and other nonsense. I was checking my bag for the afternoon's lessons and remembered I needed something in my desk, so threw the lid up. The smell that wafted up from my desk was appalling and quite shocking. From behind me I heard stifled giggles and the faint warbling of "I'm only a poor little sparrow". Inside my desk, stiff as a board, eyes glazed over and putrefaction well advanced was, indeed, a poor little, extremely dead, sparrow. Now, Edith Piaf, so named 'Little Sparrow' in her native France, may have sung "Je ne regrette rien"; I regretted not having paid closer attention to my friends and their plot.

Après-ski

There was great excitement at the start of our Year Nine with the announcement of the annual ski trip. If you've ever been skiing, you will recognise some of what is to come and, if you haven't, you still will! One of the slightly bizarre but wonderful things about Gloucester, and there are many, is that it has its very own dry slope ski run. This is where we took our first intrepid steps to prepare for the snowy slopes of Serre Chevalier in the southern Alps of France. The ski slope in Matson provided skis, ski lessons and opportunities to practise, but there the similarities between Matson and Serre Chevalier ended. Even now when I see the dry slope in Matson, it brings back fond memories that ski slope burns, and a crushed toenail caused by dropping a ski on my bare foot, cannot diminish.

After several weeks of lessons at Matson, we were primed and ready, bristling with confidence and determined to hit the slopes. Many, many hours on a coach left us with a lot of pent-up energy to burn off. This was further fuelled by packets of Anglo Bubbly, foam bananas, and Sherbet Dips that made us the bane of the coach drivers' lives as they were an absolute bugger to remove from the cracks between the coach seats. How we longed for our first sip of Orangina, sold in fabulous, bulbous glass bottles. 'Shake the bottle, free the taste.' We also relished the prospect of stocking up on Hollywood chewing gum, which we considered quite simply the coolest thing. Remember, this was 1981.

We arrived at the imaginatively named Hotel de Paris in Briancon. My three friends and I were the only Year Nine students on the trip, and all the others were from Year Ten. In those days, as is also true today, year groups didn't mix socially and there was a well-established pecking order so we wondered whether we would be treated like annoying kid sisters or taken under their wings. Time would tell.

Having dragged our cases and bags off the coach, the business of allocating rooms began. We four were to share a room with a couple of the older girls. They, of course, bagged the best beds, and we were consigned to bunk beds. We had some time before dinner and were allowed to explore the hotel. We wandered the corridors, checked out the dining room where we noted, with interest, small bottles of red wine set out for dinner...for us? With only a short time until dinner, we decided to head back to our room. We were chatting and laughing hard as we entered our room but stopped short when we became aware of a couple who were, as they say, in flagrante. What were they doing in our room and how disgusting was that? Except, of course, they weren't in our room, and we soon realised our error and backed out into the corridor and legged it, absolutely howling with laughter. We were not laughing the next day on the slopes when the couple we'd walked in on turned out to be two of our ski instructors. While I am sure they didn't hold a grudge, we wondered if that was why the one we were assigned to gave us such a tough time all week.

Other than that, the first night was fairly event-free. It turned out that the wine was for us and that was immensely exciting, even though it probably cost about one franc per bottle at the local supermarché and could have doubled as paint stripper. The novelty of eating French food, with wine and baskets of bread on the table, was fabulous and, to our unsophisticated palates, it was taste bud popping stuff.

The first day on the slopes was fun but exhausting. It turned out that the dry slope in Matson was not the preparation ground we had thought it would be and skiing in snow was a whole other challenge. It was much faster, for one thing, and made our legs ache from the resistance when snow ploughing to brake. Despite being surrounded by ice and snow, it was baking hot. We ended the day with panda faces from our ski masks and our arms up to the elbow were bronzed as they would have been after a week on a beach in the Costa del Sol. This was an added and unexpected bonus, and we were pretty chuffed with our brown bits even though we looked utterly ridiculous.

On the second day we were shattered. Muscles ached that I didn't even know I had, and skiing was rapidly turning into 'type B' fun, i.e. something you participate in which is not fun at all while doing it but, back in the comfort of your hotel, it takes on a fun quality and is fondly remembered. The sun hid behind ominous-looking clouds and the seasoned skiers muttered about "heavy falls, possibly a blizzard" heading our way. In truth, the slopes were rather bald with a lot of icy stretches that were not ideal for we ski-babies. A fresh fall of snow would be most welcome, and we wished it would come. As the saying goes, be careful what you wish for. The snow came alright and, with it, some drama.

We were skidding and falling over in ever more frequent turns and getting thoroughly frustrated. Oh, for the plastic bristles of the Matson slope. You knew where you were with a plastic bristle. Our ski instructor, he of the 'après-ski' delights, was looking more thunderous than ever and his frequent glances at the sky suggested he was worried about something. He had taken us a little higher up because the nursery slopes were little more than slush and ice and hopeless for skiing. We had found a seam of snow that at least provided something to ski on and we were getting quite good. And then, with alarming speed, the clouds came down and the weather changed. A flurry of snow soon turned into a full-scale blizzard, and our instructor directed us to form a snake with each one wrapping her arms around the waist of the girl in front. Our instructor led the snake, and we made our way, inch by inch down the mountain through snow pellets that stung our skin and pinged off our masks like bullet fire. This wasn't type B fun, it wasn't even type C fun.

We made it down in one piece and were back on the coach heading back to the hotel before you could say 'bobble hat'. Our teachers, who wore matching bobble hats, sat at the front of the coach and seemed a bit subdued. Looking back, they were probably pretty stressed about the near miss we'd had and what they would have to report back to the headmistress who was a very daunting figure. What I would say is that their problems were nothing compared to those encountered by teachers taking trips in the era of mobile phones. Had that trip taken place in 2021, parents and carers would have known about the blizzard before the second flake of snow had landed, the 'snake' would have been all over Instagram and our teachers' bobble hats would have made them TikTok superstars. Think on!

What are the dos and don'ts when choosing a residential location for a school trip? It's hard to say, but I think a hotel close to a brothel and an army barracks might not be ideal. The Hotel de Paris turned out to have both. This was not the hotel's fault, nor was it the fault of the teachers as they had little way of knowing and there was no Tripadvisor to give 'wise owl' warnings. As it turned out, blizzards, brothels and barracks were not the only risks we encountered. There were bends too.

The week of skiing was almost at an end and, for a treat and a change of scene, we were going to cross the nearby border into Italy. This was incredibly exciting and the idea that we would return home having been to two 'abroad places' was quite simply thrilling. We spent a couple of happy hours wandering around a small Italian border town, buying powdery biscuits that tasted of dust and blocks of chocolate so hard they almost dislocated your jaw. But none of that mattered because we had been to Italy and we had tasted its 'delights'. *Veni, vidi, vici.* We were in great spirits on the way back to the hotel as our ace coach drivers, who we adored, played the tunes we requested on the coach's sound system. Judging by the gentle jiggling of the bobble hats at the front of the coach, all was right with our teachers too and they turned a blind eye and ear to our music choices, despite their sometimes fruity lyrics. All was well in our world until Tony, the shift driver for the day, took a bend a little too sharply and the front wheel of the coach ended up, not so much on the road as in the air. There was a hideous moment when we hovered for a few seconds and then the coach listed to the right. "Girls, everyone needs to move over to the left-hand side now!" Tony and his co-driver Pete managed to strike just the right balance of calm and urgency, and those on the right-hand side of the coach, now with an extra clear view of the valley far below, moved silently and swiftly to sit on the laps of the girls on the left-hand side of the coach. Pete hopped out and I assume he lodged something under the wheel to fill the space between solid ground and open air. Tony revved the engine and we all held our breaths. After a few lurches and the rather stomach-churning sound of the engine straining, we were back on terra firma. A huge cheer went up and we were once again on our way. Looking back, that was probably an extremely dangerous moment and must have been terrifying for the teachers. Being teens, we soon forgot the fear part and talked about this as a huge joke. It was only in telling the story to my parents when I returned home that the penny dropped and, looking back, it probably would have been better not to have told them. As they say, what happens on tour, stays on tour.

Joy Division

At the end of Year Nine the X Division was created. This was a class of girls who sat their GCE English Literature in Year Ten and would take ten O levels instead of nine. Girls in the X Division were typically in top sets for everything. I was placed in the X Division but was in the bottom set for maths, so I had a very interesting time of it as most of the time I was in class with the most academic girls, but for maths I was with girls who struggled in most subjects. I believe I was the only girl to ever be placed in X Division who was also in the bottom set for maths. Quite an achievement, eh?

I was resistant, resentful and rebellious in my mid-teens and often fell foul of the education system. I found the approach to teaching, which involved, in the main, learning by rote and copying copious notes from the board, so utterly boring that I could have wept. Those teachers who encouraged exploration, risk-taking and independent thought were like oases in the desert and I survived the hours of silent screaming tedium by anticipating those golden lessons. Looking back, I would not have wanted to teach me when I was at my worst, and my rude, cavalier attitude to several of the staff who tried to teach me and my utter contempt for some of them, makes me cringe. Having been on the receiving end of personal remarks, withering looks and the secret language of teenage mockery, I can only now offer apologies that will never be heard. However, there is more to my story than simple teenage rebellion or moodiness. When I was in Year Nine (or the third year as we said back then), something changed at home. My parents spoke to each other in hushed voices, and a friend of theirs came to sit with me while mum went to see the GP. I remember fearing the worst and was sure that mum had cancer, but I could not bring myself to ask, because once I knew I could not unknow.

The morning after the trip to the GP, mum and dad called me into their room.

"Helen, we have something to tell you. You know your mum has been feeling a bit unwell recently. Well, the thing is, she's pregnant."

I looked at mum and back at dad. My immediate feeling was of absolute excitement and happiness. I had always wanted a sibling, but had long since given up on that idea, as I was now fourteen. The rest of the conversation is a bit of a blur, but I remember mum and dad asking me to keep this confidential for the time being and they explained that as mum was by this time approaching forty, there were tests she would have to have and well… I managed to fill in the gaps for myself.

Once mum had the all-clear, I was allowed to tell my friends. They responded in a range of ways from being excited for me, envious of the arrival of a new baby brother or sister to play with, to – not to put too fine a point on it – being horrified. I remember one of my friends looking at me and saying, "Oh my God, that means your parents are still doing it. That's gross!" That caused a few smirks and I felt horrible. Of course, I was well aware of this fact of life, but nobody really wants to dwell too much on that in relation to one's parents, and teenagers are particularly sensitive to that as they are generally getting to grips with their own sexuality, so certainly don't want to be reminded of their parents'.

This all happened a long time ago and my brother will turn forty this year. We are close and since he became a parent himself, the age gap has diminished significantly. However, looking back, I realise that the huge change from being an only child to sharing my parents with someone else definitely knocked me off course. Coupled with that, and unbeknown to me, in the autumn term I was developing glandular fever. I suspect that it is no coincidence that I entered Year Ten with an attitude that led to me being endlessly in trouble, with my parents thoroughly ashamed of me at times. I particularly remember one brutal parents' evening where my many crimes were revealed to my parents and later that same term when the headmistress hauled me over the coals in her office.

She looked at me witheringly and said, "Helen Ayling, you are a malcontent and a bad influence."

I had absolutely no idea what a malcontent was, but I knew better than to disagree, so simply nodded my head and said, "Yes, Miss."

As soon as I escaped her office, I went straight to the dictionary and looked up 'malcontent'. As I suspected, it was not a flattering description.

If this had happened today, I would probably have been assigned a mentor or equivalent to help me navigate the choppy waters I had entered and I think I would have been treated with more kindness and understanding rather than being constantly hammered. Not a single teacher asked me how I felt about having a baby brother, nobody noticed that a student who had breezed through most subjects, suddenly struggled to complete work or to concentrate in class. I was definitely drowning and not waving at that point in my school career.

The end of the fifth year came and the start of O level exams. I revised hard, filled in gaps in my learning with the fabulous revision guides that were available, prepared myself to fail maths, as C was the lowest pass grade in the O level and my mock exam results suggested that a D would be a minor miracle. What I hadn't really factored in was periods. It wasn't that I hadn't started my periods or that I wasn't used to managing them but, when mine kicked in right at the start of one of my two-hour Chemistry O level papers, well, let me put it this way, it was not ideal, and I was totally unprepared. Despite attending an all-girls' school, it was still a source of great embarrassment for anyone to know that you were having a period and, so, I did the only logical thing; I sat tight, said nothing, and bled through my underwear and summer uniform dress. The cramps made me feel nauseous but the thought of the walk of shame that awaited me when I got out of my seat and had to walk out of the hall in a mess, was even worse. When the exam ended, I did my best to disguise my plight by tying my cardigan tightly around my waist. I shuffled out of the exam hall and tried to work out how the hell I would make it home in this state. I had to face a thirty-minute bus ride, followed by a fifteen-minute walk before I was safely home. I don't remember much about the ordeal except for stuffing my undies with paper towels in an attempt to improvise a sanitary towel and rustling all the way to the bus. This may sound utterly ridiculous, but the shame and fear of discovery was such that I was prepared to go through physical and mental contortions to avoid exposure at all costs, particularly in front of the boys from the grammar school next door who caught the same bus.

It is curious how some memories come to the fore. I had completely forgotten about this incident until I started writing. There was a lot of fear and shame woven through school life for girls and I am glad that so many of those stigmas have, at least in part, been lifted. But I also know that other pressures have replaced those that we wrestled with in the 1970s and 1980s. I can't say which are worse.

The end of formal exams was always celebrated with gusto and our year was no exception, although we went just a little bit further. My extended group of friends hatched two plans. One involved bringing booze into school to toast the end of exams and the other was to jump, fully dressed in our uniforms, into the canal. Neither idea was sensible, neither was well thought through and neither went well! I can still see the ambulance making its way onto the school grounds to scoop up one of my friends who had consumed most of a bottle of Southern Comfort and now lay flat on her back on the playing field in full sight of the teachers. The paramedics attended to her and carted her off to receive treatment. Happily, she was none the worse for this, but it was, ironically, a sobering experience. So much for plan A. Plan B also ended in disaster. One friend leaped with great enthusiasm into the canal, and we all whooped with excitement. But excitement soon turned to fear as she emerged with blood pouring profusely from her leg, having cut it on what was probably a discarded bottle lurking at the bottom of the canal.

Strangely, I have no recollection of what happened next, but I know she was alright in the end and, judging by lively Facebook posts from both of these former schoolmates to this very day, neither suffered any lasting damage from their misadventures!

I was much happier in sixth form and chose subjects I loved and could really get to grips with. As an agnostic with the ambition to 'graduate' to atheism, I chose Religious Studies, which did not disappoint, History and English Literature. I worked hard, read around my subjects, got fully involved in wider school life and became Vice Captain of a pastoral house, with one of my dearest friends as House Captain. We organised treasure hunts, house plays and other activities for the enjoyment of our peers and the younger girls in our house. Given that this was an all-girls' grammar school, you might expect that the houses would be named after inspirational women. Ours were named after alpha males – Winston Churchill, Mohandas Gandhi, John F Kennedy and Robert Falcon Scott. I was in Churchill House but knew very little about the man himself. I found out a paltry amount and then cared even less. I had always wanted to be in Gandhi House as he, at least, seemed to have had values I sympathised with; he wasn't some boring white bloke and he wasn't about striding around the globe, kicking its ass into submission. In fact, one of my favourite stories about Gandhi is that he came to Gloucestershire to visit the Whiteway Colony, a socialist residential community that was uber-cool in its day. The story goes that Gandhi bought his famous round glasses from an optician in Gloucester. As a well-travelled adult, I have fallen back in love with Gloucester, but as a teen, I would have been incredulous at the idea of anyone so famous visiting Gloucester rather than the 'thinking man's Gloucester', i.e. Cheltenham. I get it now and if Gandhi was alive today I'd direct him to Barton Street in Gloucester rather than the High Street in Cheltenham.

I was to have a further tricky encounter with the headmistress, Miss Boreham, who had, early in my career as a secondary school student, informed me that I was a malcontent. I was summoned to her office one day and sat outside, waiting for the little traffic light sign next to her door to turn green, the signal to enter and receive a grilling.

The sign vibrated, the light turned green, and in I went.

"Sit," she said.

I sat.

"Do you know why I have asked to see you?"

"No, Miss Boreham."

"I want you to apply to Oxford to study Theology."

There was no preamble. This was not a dialogue, and I was cornered. What does a person do when cornered? Submit, hide or fight back? You can probably guess what I did. It did not go well.

"Thank you, Miss Boreham, but I really want to study English Literature and I am looking at Liverpool as one of my choices."

"Liverpool?" she said in a tone not unlike that of the famous 'handbag' line uttered by Lady Bracknell. "So, you are saying no to applying to Oxford?"

"Yes, Miss Boreham."

"Very well. You may go."

I was dispatched without further ado. I felt quite pleased with myself and went back to tell my friends about this latest encounter with our formidable headmistress. That was the end of the matter. Or so I thought.

It was after my third university rejection letter that my parents and I started to become perplexed. I was doing well in my subjects, my conduct was, in the main, good and I was playing an active role in wider school life. In the end, the only university to offer me an interview was Liverpool. The good news was that I was keen to go there, but rejections from all the other universities was worrying. As teachers themselves, my parents knew all too well what an absolute pain pushy parents could be, so they rarely contacted my teachers. There was conjecture about the reference from my head of sixth form and, of course, as mum acknowledged, I had turned down the headmistress's express wish that I try for Oxford. We never did find out the truth of the matter, but it left an unpleasant and lingering question in my mind. Was I effectively blackballed?

Paddy's Wigwam

To say that Liverpool in the 1980s was simply the most fantastic place to study and live would be an understatement. I loved everything about Liverpool, and it remains my favourite 'other home' to this day. True, it was a city scarred from riots that had ripped apart buildings and communities and the evidence of that was clear and shocking. On the bus ride from our halls of residence to the university, we passed blackened buildings, boarded-up shops and windows that still wore protective bars. And yet, for all that, something about the beauty and energy of the city just couldn't be crushed, and thank God for that. I would liken Liverpool to Havana as both are cities of immense beauty which wear their scars, if not proudly, then at least not with shame.

Much has already been written about the humour, the music and the spirit of the city and its people so I won't go where others have already trodden, but I want to share what I consider to be a brilliant example of Liverpudlian humour. Catching a cab back from town one evening with two friends, we tried to explain to the driver that we wanted to be dropped off by the Catholic cathedral.

"Oh, youse want Paddy's Wigwam. Why didn't youse say?"

Now, if you have visited Liverpool or even seen a picture of this cathedral, you will get the joke. If not, check it out!

My path to university was not exactly smooth, so what I am about to share will probably not come as a great surprise. I am embarrassed to admit this, but I have committed to an honest account of my life, so here goes. I was determined to study English Literature and had found a range of universities that delivered what looked to be excellent courses. As grammar school gals we were firmly nudged towards Russell Group universities and I dutifully, and exclusively, applied to those. I remember leafing through the UCCA book, poring over the courses and entry requirements. I completed my application and sent it off. So how on earth did I manage to make such a monumental cock-up? For some reason, and I will never fathom how this happened, I had applied to study English Language and Literature rather than straight Literature and, even more embarrassingly, it wasn't until I rocked up to an Anglo-Saxon session involving full-on language labs, headphones, the works, that I realised my error. However, it was, as it turned out, a most fortuitous error as I loved the language aspects of the course and learned so much about how English evolved. The Anglo-Saxon poems we studied were absolute corkers and some of the riddles were scandalously rude, especially one about a young woman pulling a large onion from the ground. The description of its purple head and her enthusiastic grasping of said 'head' sent us into fits of giggles and I will leave it with you to work out the implied meaning of that riddle!

Life in Liverpool was never dull. Looking back, we certainly encountered some risky situations but came away pretty much unscathed. My friend Sally and I once went to do the weekly supermarket shop. We decided that a taxi was the best way to get ourselves and our bags of shopping back to Mossley Hill. We hailed a black cab and hopped in. It wasn't until we had been in the cab for a few minutes that we realised that the driver was not the person whose ID badge was displayed on the grill. We weren't too concerned and thought that perhaps it was a shared cab. But when the driver ignored two sets of directions from us and hit an alarming speed well in excess of the local speed limit, we started to feel scared. We looked at each other, rolled our eyes and gripped the seat with both hands as the cab lurched deeper into the city and in the opposite direction to where we were supposed to be going.

I tried once more to ask the driver to drop us off. He ignored us, but the look he gave us in the mirror is something I will never forget. He almost snarled at us and put his foot down even harder. What were we to do and where was he taking us? We were in no mood to hang about and find out. Sally whispered, "At the next lights when the door locks are released, let's jump out and leg it." We prepared to do just that and, when the opportunity came, we rolled out of the cab, shopping bags in hand, and ran as fast as we could. Looking back, I think we were in very real danger, and I thank Sally to this day for her cool head in a crisis.

Our first year in halls was lovely. Mossley Hill, a suburb to the south of the city, was a great place to be and the local residents were used to students and not antagonised by them. We were very protected in many ways and didn't have the domestic chores that came with living in a student house. However, shopping, cooking for ourselves and budgeting were all novel and exciting concepts and we were keen to spread our wings.

At the start of my second year, I moved into a student house in Anfield with my friends Liz, Sally and Tim. Our move to our new house did not have a very auspicious start. In order to secure the house on Canon Road, we had paid a retainer of half the weekly rent for the summer. When we viewed the house, we thought it would do nicely. It was in reasonable order and had four fair-sized bedrooms. Liz and I arranged to meet up at the house during the summer holidays to check that all was well and to drop some stuff off. We arrived from Nottingham and Stroud, respectively, and hugged enthusiastically when we met at Lime Street Station. We jumped on the 14C Croxteth bus, known as the 'smack bus', to Anfield. It was called the smack bus for good reason and, on more occasions than I wish to remember, we saw youngsters 'chasing the dragon' – using strips of kitchen foil to burn heroin and then inhaling the smoke. It was a tragic sight.

Liz and I arrived at the house on Canon Road and knocked on the door to let the landlord know we had arrived. We heard the sound of children's voices and a rather harassed-looking young woman arrived at the door.

"What do youse want?" she asked.

"We've come to drop our stuff off. We're moving in next month."

"I don't bloody think so. We live here. Now get lost!"

With that, she slammed the door shut and Liz and I were left confused, perplexed and increasingly angry. What the hell was going on? Where was the landlord and, more to the point, where on earth were we going to live? Just as we were really starting to panic, there was a screech of brakes, and a flashy car came to a stop next to us. Was this our landlord we wondered?

"Alright, girls!" It was indeed the landlord.

We explained that no, we were not alright and asked who was living in our house?

"Don't you worry, girls. I've got somewhere much better for you just round the corner. Hop in."

We were so gobsmacked that we dutifully hopped in and were soon hurtling down Canon Road, around the corner and onto Chapel Road to a house that the Addams Family would have loved and not because it was a Gothic mansion. The house was dark and dingy, with cobwebs adorning every corner. Liz and I looked at each other and silently agreed that we would just have to lump it. Why didn't we put up more of a fight? Why did we just roll over and accept this shabby treatment? Simple really. We were only nineteen and twenty and didn't have the experience to manage a wily landlord.

October arrived and we installed ourselves in the 'palace' that was Chapel Road. It was grim, but we made the best of it and managed to have some fun times there despite the cherry knocking by local kids who were fascinated by students. We got to know the local area and its amenities, such as they were. When Liverpool played at home, our road became an extended car park, and we could hear the roar of the crowd from our living room.

One evening on our way back from a night out, we dropped into our local chippy. When we came out, we were met with a truly shocking sight. A man, probably in his late thirties, was tottering around outside the chippy. His top was covered in blood, and he was clearly worse for wear, but didn't appear to be injured. We just stood staring at him, like rabbits caught in the headlights. He spotted us through his alcohol haze and took a few stumbling steps towards us. If we had had any sense, we would have legged it and called the police, but we were rooted to the spot, fascinated by the scene in front of us.

"Youse lot, what you staring at?"

"Nothing. Are you ok, mate? Do you need an ambulance?" Tim my flatmate asked.

This question was greeted by incoherent mumbling and, with a shake of his head, the man seemed to fire off a synapse that cleared his brain for just long enough for him to inform us, "I've just murdered someone."

Ye gads! This was too much information and we turned on our heels and ran as fast as we could back to the safety and relative sanctuary of Chapel Road. We never found out if he had killed somebody or not, but judging by the state of him, it was clear that something very serious had occurred. This was back in 1986 so you will forgive me if my recollections are somewhat hazy. I think one of us phoned the police and reported the incident, but I couldn't say what the outcome was. It was an incident that we often talked about and recalled with a shudder.

Life as a student in Anfield was pretty challenging which is why most sensible students didn't live there. I mean no disrespect to the past or current residents of Anfield but, back in 1986, students in that part of town were generally viewed with suspicion, seen as 'posh' and not really welcomed. It was assumed that we were all rich and so it wasn't long before we became a target for burglars. My experience of burglary as a student was a bit different to what you might imagine.

There was a small yard with a washing line at the back of our house. We also had one of those Dutch dryers that could be hoisted up in the kitchen. We only used it when the weather was bad but, given our diet of cigarettes and fry-ups, the clothes often smelled worse after they had been dried on that, so, when the weather was a little more clement, the washing line swung into action. As a student, I had little money for nice clothes, with the exception of a navy blue and white striped jumper from Next that was my pride and joy. It was my turn to use the washing line and so I pegged out the jumper, my duvet cover, pillowcases and sheet. I had a pet hamster who had lived in a cage under my bed the previous year in defiance of halls of residence rules. While living under my bed, he had chewed a hole in the corner of the duvet when it dangled temptingly through the bars of his cage. The duvet remained my favourite bedding, despite the hole. I also hung out my ripped jeans, which were the height of fashion in Liverpool in the 1980s. I smile today when I see youngsters wearing the same style as they no doubt think they've invented this fashion.

I left my washing to dry and went off to lectures without any further thought. When I returned to Chapel Road later that afternoon, I saw that the line was empty and thought how kind it was of Sally, Liz or Tim to have brought my washing in.

"Guys, thank you!" I called up the stairs.

"Thanks for what?" Sally called down from her room.

"For getting my washing in."

"Eh? What washing? I didn't see any washing?"

Then the penny dropped. All of my washing, even the duvet with the hole, had been nicked off the washing line. I could have wept for that lovely Next jumper. That was the last time I used that wretched washing line and until the end of the year, had to resign myself to clothes and bedding that smelled of fry-ups and fags. Why not use the local launderette, I hear you ask? Frankly, after encounters with heroin users, murderers, dodgy landlords and the local cherry knockers, visiting the launderette seemed a step too far.

We were not sorry to say farewell to Chapel Road when things came to a head when we returned from our Christmas holidays in January 1987. We were greeted by burst pipes in the kitchen that had sprayed water down the wall which had frozen into an admittedly rather beautiful ice mural. The house was bone-chillingly cold and, when the electricity went one night, we were obliged to sleep in a huddle of duvets and blankets on the living room floor. We decided enough was enough. The next day we packed our belongings, called two cabs and left without a backward glance. We shoved the keys through the letterbox and left a note for the landlord informing him that we were leaving with immediate effect. At the students' union, student services were extremely helpful and got us straight back into the very same halls of residence we'd been in the year before. They placed the landlord on a blacklist to prevent other students from falling foul of his dodgy antics. That experience taught us some important lessons, not least about contracts, legal rights and how to be more assertive. One day, many months later, Liz, Sally and I were out strolling in Mossley Hill when we heard a familiar voice calling to us from the wound-down window of a familiar-looking flashy car.

"You alright, girls? You got that rent you owe me?"

Emboldened by our experience and the lessons we had learned, we informed him that a) he had taken money from us for a property he had already rented out, b) Chapel Road was dangerous and not fit for living in, and c) we were not paying him a single penny more, so he could go whistle.

He just laughed and said, "Fair enough. See youse." And with that, he was off with a jaunty toot of his horn and blare of music.

We giggled all the way back to halls and often recalled this encounter.

All good things must come to an end and so it was with my Liverpool days. I remember those three years with immense fondness. I am so glad that I had that time, in that special city, at that particular time in its history.

It's got quite a nice service station

1988 marked the end of one academic chapter and the beginning of the next. I was very much in love and chose where to study for an MA based on wanting to be with my boyfriend. This is not, of course, a sound basis for choosing a university, but I daresay I wasn't the first to do so, nor would I be the last. My beloved at the time was studying Law at North Staffordshire Poly, so I chose the University of Keele. Keele's reputation was not what it is now and most people only knew about it because it had quite nice motorway services. In all honesty, I used to wince when people asked where I studied for my Masters and I could anticipate their looks of surprise when I told them that I had attended the esteemed Russell Group University of Liverpool and then chosen... well... Keele. This was the snobbery that existed in those days and, of course, there was still the great divide between the unis and the polys, which was a whole other ball game. In fact, the course at Keele was excellent and was exactly what I wanted to do, so from that point of view, I lost nothing at all by going there and, of course, it meant that I could move into a place with my boyfriend and that was exciting.

My year in Staffordshire was very enjoyable. I learned about The Potteries and the rhythm of the year created by work patterns in the local factories. I took on two jobs to pay the rent and bills and met some lovely folk while working at a local vegetarian and vegan restaurant, which was quite a brave venture in the middle of Hanley, Stoke-on-Trent, in 1988. I also…drum roll…worked as a 'Leisure Professional' for Staffordshire's most famous employer, Alton Towers. The employee benefits were, of course, considerable, but really what topped it off for my boyfriend and I was the opportunity to ride any rollercoaster we wanted as many times as we wanted before our shift began in the morning. As you will appreciate, riding a rollercoaster at 8.30 in the morning is not for the faint-hearted and certainly not to be recommended after a heavy night out. But it was an exciting way to kick-start the day and beats Pilates or Tai Chi for getting one in the mood to tackle Joe Public, or 'Joes' as we fondly referred to the park's guests.

Now if that wasn't enough excitement, imagine the Disney World-style parade that took place every afternoon with a host of lovable characters, including Henry and Henrietta Hound, the park's mascots. I loved the parade and each day I watched it weaving its way through the park, past the Tower gift shop, the Black Hole rollercoaster and the Log Flume, all of which I worked at over the months. I dreamed of being in the parade but, as a mere Leisure Professional, it was not for me, and I could only look on with envy as my colleagues from the 'Ents team' paraded past each day. What I learned from them, however, was that such was the tedium of parading day after day that after about the twentieth time, they would rather gouge their own eyes out than ever parade again. But to me it looked like great fun and certainly beat dishing out sick bags to green-about-the-gills guests as they disembarked the Black Hole rollercoaster.

Reader, my dream came true! One day the call came, and I was ready to answer it. Someone on the Ents team was sick and this left the park short of a Henrietta Hound for the parade. I was in there quicker than you could say 'Houndtastic' and was whisked off to the Ents area where I was given my costume. I hadn't factored in that the usual wearer of the suit was quite tall and I am not. When I turned to admire my new furry form in the mirror, I was dismayed to find that the suit came down to the ground and where Henrietta's legs should have been, there were just large feet. It would have to do. I was hoisted aloft my steed – a large, fibreglass swan. I kid you not. So far, so good. I held tight to the swan's neck and my float lurched forward. We had to wave to the crowds as we travelled around the park and that seemed straightforward enough. I could just about see out of the eye grill in the head of the suit, but I couldn't see very clearly. No matter, I would be the most enthusiastic waver and I set to my task with gusto. All was going well; I was enjoying myself immensely and possibly got a tad overexcited. The float gave an unexpected lurch and I felt, with a prickle of fear, my furry hands begin to lose their grip on the swan's neck. With each bump and judder, I slowly but surely slid round the neck until I was left hanging on underneath the neck for dear life and dignity. I must have made for a very strange sight indeed as the other Henrys and Henriettas maintained their vertical postures and I alone swung and flailed from my swan. Perhaps there were no further absences from the Ents team, but I was never asked to play Henrietta Hound again. Their loss!

Those who can, teach!

Having completed my Masters at Keele, it was time to turn my attention to something vocational and so I applied for teacher training. The PGCE course at King's College, London, was excellent and I was extremely fortunate to have such inspiring tutors. The course struck the right balance between academic research and practical experience, and I thoroughly enjoyed that year. The only fly in the ointment was the department's rather strange way of allocating our teaching practice schools, as it certainly bore no relation to where we lived in London. My first school placement was to be three bus rides away in Hounslow which, by my calculation, would have taken close to three hours each way. Fortunately, my tutor agreed that this was impractical, and a new placement was found for me at an all-girls' school in Wimbledon. Ah ha, I thought to myself, a cushy little number. Thank you, that will do nicely!

I arrived on my first day, bristling with lesson plans and enthusiasm. How hard could this be? Compared to some of my fellow students, I had fallen on my feet. Wimbledon is posh, I thought, and the girls will be keen, attentive and eager to learn. Had I learned nothing from my own experience as a student at a middle-class all-girl's grammar school? We were capable of monstrous behaviour and obnoxious attitudes. What on earth made me think that my new charges would be any different? Except that they were different. They were streetwise, unimpressed and not from Wimbledon. While Wimbledon is indeed a very leafy and charming part of London, my girls took the bus or Tube from further afield. They were tough, cynical and could eat me for breakfast.

One of my classes was 10X and I sensed that I was being, if not actually set up, then at least tested. I had already twigged that this 10X would be nothing like the 10X I had been in myself as a teen. The head of department looked a bit distracted when she went through my timetable with me, something I put down to her having other pressing matters on her mind, like her imminent maternity leave.

"There are some characters in this class," she said. "But once you show them who is boss, they'll be fine."

I nodded sagely and hoped I looked more confident than I felt. How on earth would I get them to see me as the person in charge and what exactly did she mean by 'characters'?

My plans for the first lesson were checked and given the green light, but nothing could have prepared me for the next hour. I still laugh and shudder at the memory. The class awaited me, but not expectantly as I had anticipated. In fact, when I addressed them, their conversations barely dipped a decibel and, giving me a quick up and down look, they carried on as before. I wasn't worth worrying about and they clearly didn't see me as someone of interest or relevance. I walked to the board at the front of the room, put my bag on the floor and turned to face the girls. I waited, they ignored me, I started to feel irritated and they…ignored me some more.

"Good morning, 10X. My name is Miss Ayling, and I am going to be your teacher this term."

"You're a student teacher, innit."

This was a rhetorical question and my first encounter with that most multifunctional linguistic gem, 'innit'. Panic! What should I say? If I admitted my amateur status, they would surely take advantage, but if I pretended to a level of experience I didn't have, I would also come a cropper. I chose to ignore the question and press on with the lesson.

"Ok, girls, we are going to be studying poetry this term and I've chosen one I think you'll find interesting. It's about a woman in prison."

I whipped out my pre-prepared resources which consisted of worksheets produced on a Banda machine. Maybe you've never heard of a Banda machine, or maybe you are feeling nostalgic right now for the purple-tinted hands and smell of meths that came with using and cleaning the machine. I was very proud of my worksheet. I had illustrated it myself with a cartoon figure in a stripy prison uniform. Good job I was impressed by it, because nobody else was. A couple of girls picked up their sheets, glanced at them and then went right back to their far more interesting conversation.

By now, my heart was beating fast, I was flushed in the face, and I was feeling well and truly out of my depth, and the hour had only begun. Like a cat with a mouse, 10X were only playing with me at this stage and I had yet to experience the full horrors they were capable of. Somehow, we got started and a few of the girls were kind enough or perhaps bored enough to have a go at the poem and the activities I had set up. Getting any kind of response was like drawing blood from the proverbial, but I pressed on. After about twenty minutes of pretty torturous exchanges, the classroom door opened and a large girl ambled in. The first thing I noticed was her lilac eyeshadow. She stopped in her tracks when she saw me, looked me up and down with disdain, gave a long slow thoughtful chew on her gum and then ambled over to her desk.

"Good morning," I said. "You are rather late. What's your name so I can add you to the register?"

She looked at me through haughty lilac lids and then turned back to her friends.

"She's called Ursula, Miss," one of the more helpful girls eagerly informed me.

"Ok, Ursula, can you explain why you're so late?"

Ursula looked me up and down again. "Cos I am, innit."

I sort of gave up at that point and calculated swiftly that more time spent on this issue would result in less time cracking on with poetry, so I nodded and turned my attention to a group of girls who had got stuck with one of the tasks. Ten minutes passed and I felt on a roll. Nothing disastrous was happening, the girls were not rioting and, frankly, apart from Ursula's tardiness and tendency to do absolutely nothing, this was all going rather well. What exactly was all the fuss about 10X?

Oh, how foolish I was. I had walked right into the trap that they had cunningly laid for me. Thus far, Ursula had spent the lesson slumped in her chair, a nail file industriously employed, but not a pen in sight. And then something extraordinary happened. Ursula put her hand up. At last, I thought, I've got her hooked and even Ursula cannot resist my Banda worksheet forever.

"Miss, can I ask you something?"

"Of course, Ursula. Fire away."

"Miss, do you always talk out of your fu**ing ar*e?"

Well, what does one say to that? Strange though it may seem, I did nothing about this and just put it down to an unpleasant but necessary type of experience. I did feel pretty rattled but was so out of my depth, I just did my best to press on.

Days became weeks and my teaching practice was nearing the halfway mark. I would like to tell you that I had 10X under control by now, but I didn't, and every lesson was a battle of wills in which they often beat me hands down. 10Y, on the other hand, were an absolute delight and we were cracking on with *To Kill A Mockingbird* with great success. They were engaged, inquisitive and willing to give me a fair shot at practising my teaching skills on them. My three younger classes were also fine and pretty soon forgot that I was new to the profession. I told myself that having four out of five classes more or less on track wasn't bad and perhaps I should accept that this was as good as it was going to get. However, rather like the parable of the ninety-nine sheep, it was the one sheep or, in my case, 10X, that really had me fretting and I couldn't rest until I had them progressing as they should.

Each week I had a meeting with my in-school mentor. The head of department had this role until she took maternity leave three weeks into my teaching practice, and I was now mentored by the deputy head of department. She was a cool customer, not very friendly and a bit intimidating, as she had effortless control over her classes, was a mistress of withering sarcasm and was clearly irritated by student teachers or perhaps just by me. We talked through my plans for the next half term, she gave me tips on behaviour management and then asked me in a way that suggested she hoped that the answer would be "no," whether I had any concerns with my classes. Was this the moment to mention Ursula? I wasn't sure but thought, what the hell, I had nothing to lose. I told her about the "fu**ing ar*e" comment. She looked at me with what I can only describe as incredulity.

"She said what?"

I repeated Ursula's rhetorical gem.

"And you didn't think to report that to me?"

I was confused. Was I in trouble now? I didn't understand. Seeing how crestfallen I must have looked, my mentor softened a little and explained that a) I absolutely shouldn't tolerate such rudeness, b) there was a behaviour policy that I could and should use to support my classroom management and c) she would be having a word in the shell-like of Miss Ursula!

Those of you who have ever taught may also be wondering why I didn't report this incident at the time or why I didn't deal with it. With regard to the former, the issue was pride, and I didn't even want to admit that a pupil had felt they could speak to me like that. And I didn't deal with it because of inexperience. In fact, nobody had thought to go through the school's behaviour policy with me and, as there had been no handover between my mentors, I had fallen between two stools, so to speak. I don't blame them for this and actually, in many ways, I have Ursula to thank for a much better relationship developing with my second mentor as she supported me fully with 10X after that revelation, taught me a lot about classroom management and sent me on my way with high expectations regarding behaviour in my future classrooms and schools.

The Great Egg Race

Do you remember The Great Egg Race? It ran from 1979 until 1986 and was extremely popular. The idea was to challenge teams of inventors to build gadgets from limited resources that could carry eggs the furthest distance possible. It was a weird but engaging concept. During the second half of my teaching practice in Wimbledon, some bright spark suggested that the girls would love to have a go at this and, so, a day of egg race type activities was planned for Year Ten. There was a lot of discussion in the staffroom with views polarised between those who thought it was a total waste of time and those who couldn't wait to get stuck in. I fell into the latter camp as I was a keenie beanie and had a liking for activities or excursions that would break up the monotony of a typical working week. I was also intrigued to see how the characters in 10X would respond to this challenge and was especially interested to see how Ursula got on.

There was a set of identical twins in Year Ten who were, not to put too fine a point on it, notorious. They came as a unit, each was as unruly as the other and staff were terrified of them. One of them was in 10X. Occasionally, they'd drop in on each other's lessons or sometimes swap places, just for the sheer hell of it. It was almost impossible to identify them when seen separately and they played that to its full advantage.

The morning of The Great Egg Race dawned and there was a definite air of expectation when I arrived at school. Year Ten were to be released from their normal timetabled lessons and the staff who were due to teach them would supervise their activities in the main hall. So far, so good. To be perfectly honest, I was quite relieved to have a bit of a reprieve from actually trying to teach them and I figured that there would be safety in numbers with plenty of staff in the hall to jointly supervise the Year Tens. Ah, the naivety of the rookie teacher.

Year Ten was not known for its compliance at the best of times, although there were, of course, lots of lovely students who were keen, engaged and well behaved. Individually, most of the girls were great. Organised into classes, they could be won around. But when they came together as a year group, it was like the scene from *Gremlins* when water is dropped onto the docile Mogwai.

As the Year Ten classes were brought to the hall, they were put into groups of twelve around circular tables. Each group was supplied with a box of eggs, five potatoes, a large box of matches and two sharp kitchen knives. The first challenge was to create a bridge using the potatoes and the matches that was of sufficient strength to roll the eggs along it without breaking either the eggs or the bridge. This was quite a challenge, and we were curious to see how the girls would tackle the problem.

What unfolded still shocks me, despite the more than thirty-year gap between that day and the present. I think if your experience of school is based solely on being a pupil, then what I am about to describe will seem like fiction and something that could not possibly happen. But I am afraid it could, and it did.

The first twenty minutes or so passed uneventfully with the odd bit of banter between the girls and the staff, and the atmosphere was generally chirpy. If staff were pleased to have a break from teaching, the girls were even more pleased to have a break from being taught. Some ingenious bridges began to emerge and it was already clear that it was going to be a tough call to determine the three winners. A couple of groups struggled to get going and their bridges were in danger of resulting in scrambled eggs, but they seemed to be enjoying themselves, nonetheless.

Some smart soul had decided to put the twins in the same group (or maybe they had joined forces unbidden). Even I knew that divide and conquer was the best policy with those two. However, so far, they were behaving quite well so it was a case of not kicking that particular hornets' nest. And that hornets' nest would have been fine had it not been for the wasp. As every teacher knows, wasps are the Devil's helpers in striped form. The single buzz of a passing wasp can cause anarchy in a usually compliant class, so you can imagine the impact of a wasp buzzing through a packed hall filled with an entire year group. Many a lesson has been rendered undeliverable because of a wasp and, even as a very inexperienced trainee teacher, I knew this was not going to end well.

The shrieks began as soon as the wasp was spotted and the girls began turning over their chairs in excitement and exaggerated horror. The staff tried in vain to calm them and tempers became frayed. My instincts told me to track the twins because if there was trouble brewing they were sure to be fanning the flames. Sure enough, they were, but worse. Much worse. Each twin held a knife in her hand which she threw in the general direction of the wasp. I have no doubt that they knew there was absolutely no possibility of hitting a wasp at such a distance, and I also have no doubt that their actions were calculated to cause maximum disruption and, last but not least, they knew they were in control. The situation rapidly deteriorated and soon several girls were throwing knives. This was frightening, dangerous and took us all by surprise. We tried to gain control of the hall, but it was too late and, between the hysteria, the heady excitement of what was becoming a coup and the adrenaline coursing through everyone's veins, we found ourselves in the midst of what can only be described as a riot.

There is no happy ending to this story. There were no heroes but, thankfully, neither were there victims. A 999 call was put out. We were instructed to lock all exits out of the hall so that the girls couldn't run out and to await the arrival of the police. Mercifully, they arrived swiftly, although the intervening minutes had felt like hours. The police dealt with the incident and left, and the ringleaders were led away to the head's office to be informed of their fate. We all felt pretty wobbly afterwards and the thought of what might have happened was sobering.

Looking back, it seems utterly mad that the students had been given sharp knives, but knives and other sharp tools were used in a number of practical subjects, so perhaps it is understandable when seen in that context. Sadly, what had been intended as a challenging and engaging activity turned into an ugly incident that left its mark on us all.

Something I learned from the Ursula incident was not to sit on things that concerned me and so I contacted my tutor to talk through this alarming turn of events. She was very shocked indeed and immediately phoned the head teacher who confirmed my version of events, conceded that there had been a breakdown in behaviour at the school and said that she would understand if I preferred to complete my teaching practice elsewhere. I weighed things up and decided, on balance, that I preferred to stay where I was. I learned many hard lessons during my placement in Wimbledon but probably the most valuable was not to give up when faced with tough situations. That stood me in good stead in the years to come.

Stranger than fiction

After two placements, my fellow student teachers and I were deemed ready to assume employment as teachers and, so, in June 1990, I attended a 'pool interview' with Wandsworth Local Education Authority (LEA). Mine was the last year to train under the former Inner London Education Authority (ILEA) and I always wished that I had taught under ILEA too as its legacy of creativity, fabulous resourcing and energy were still evident when I started my first post. In those days, you applied to an LEA and were placed in a school. This is an alien concept to most new generations of teachers, except for those academy chains and Multi Academy Trusts (MATs) where there is a degree of flexibility in moving teachers from school to school as needed. The most common way for a teacher to seek a post now would be to apply directly to a school and they would expect to be employed by that organisation.

I was appointed as an English teacher at Southfields Community College, a largish comprehensive school on the edge of Wandsworth. It was a fabulous school for me. It was tough enough to cut my behaviour teeth on but not so challenging that I couldn't actually teach. There was a thriving sixth form, and I was delighted to be given an A level group in my first year. I was only twenty-three and my students were seventeen and eighteen. That was a tiny age gap and I remember some real showdowns with a couple of the lads who demanded to know my credentials for teaching them. Once this was settled and they realised I had something useful to teach them, we became a very tight unit and I remember them fondly to this day. Back then, we taught a fabulous syllabus which was 100% coursework that allowed for a lot of creativity. I remember taking A level Art and English Literature students to see a Rothko exhibition. One of my students was so inspired by this and by the stream of consciousness literature that I had introduced to the group that he produced one coursework piece as a stream of consciousness that included painting and written text. His coursework was awarded the highest mark in the country by the Associated Examining Board (AEB).

Memories of Southfields remain with me to this day, and I met such good folk there. One former colleague has remained a close friend and we reminisce about the funny and bizarre things that happened, such as the day our school was used to film scenes from the television police drama *The Bill*. Like other locations in south-west London, the school was occasionally used for this purpose. When a gritty-looking school backdrop was required, production needed to look no further than Southfields. On this particular day, we were a bit grumpy. A scene was being filmed in the staffroom, so we'd been kicked out and asked to use the main hall instead. As some sort of compensation, we were to be catered for by the production caterers, who kept the cast and crew in sausage baps and the like. However, we were not overly impressed when we came down for morning break to find a motley assortment of snacks set out, including crab sticks. Yuck!

Break was well underway when one of the deputy heads suddenly came rushing into the hall, looking panicked. "Everyone out now. I need you to clear the playground."

One brave soul piped up, "But it's not even the end of break and I haven't finished my coffee."

The deputy head turned round and almost spat out, "I said now. Don't argue, just do it!"

We sensed something was up, so we grumpily shuffled out to the main playground. Now, if it is hard to get teachers out of a staffroom or, in this case, temporary staffroom, before the end of break, you just try clearing a playground full of pupils who know they still have ten minutes of break left. It was a less than ideal scenario. But, somehow, we managed to get everyone back into their classrooms, deal with stragglers and quiet the moans and groans. My classroom overlooked the back field but colleagues who taught on the playground side of the building later explained what unfolded.

It transpired that while filming was going on, a sixth form student had stabbed a Year Ten student. The knife wound to his lower back had narrowly missed one of his kidneys. The young man was taken swiftly to the admin office where a trained first-aider laid him on the floor and applied pressure to the wound until the paramedics arrived. Two ambulances attended the scene and, for a truly bizarre few minutes, *The Bill* actors, dressed as police, mingled with the real police and paramedics on the playground. Staff who saw the ambulances and police assumed this was part of the filming. I doubt the cast experienced anything like it before or since. It still seems unreal, even as I describe it now. The young man was taken to hospital and made a full recovery. His assailant was dealt with by the police. It was a very sobering incident. I remember watching that episode of *The Bill* when it aired and shuddering at the thought of how that day's filming might have ended.

A day at the seaside

I am old enough to remember when the summer term was a lovely, relaxed time. Once Year Eleven and Thirteen finished their exams, the school took on a very different atmosphere and the staffroom was alive with the sound of laughter and banter. We planned interesting trips and cross-curricular projects, marking went to the wall for a few weeks and everyone relaxed. Happy days!

Trips out were a big part of the summer term calendar, and these were planned well in advance but without anything like the neurotic level of detail and health and safety paranoia that you find these days. We had a pragmatic but robust approach to these trips and inexperienced staff were always supported and led by the old hands and given time to learn the ropes. If something went wrong, which was almost inevitable with teenagers in tow, it was dealt with calmly and without drama. Unlike today, incidents weren't broadcast on social media and teachers, rather than parents, called the shots. These days, with Facebook, Instagram, YouTube, and so on, the level of scrutiny, opportunities to blow things out of proportion and an unhealthy desire to share every last detail with the world, means that taking students on trips and residentials has become like running the gauntlet and, in some school settings, the level of parental pressure is almost unbearable.

This was to be my first experience of taking a year group out for the day and I was looking forward to it. I was to join my Year Nine tutor group along with the rest of that year's tutors and groups. I was very fond of my group, even though they had given me the runaround at first. The kids were very excited about our planned day out in Southend. I had never been to Southend, so I didn't know what to expect. My tutor group, however, assured me that it would be "det", which I knew was praise indeed.

We walked in an enormous crocodile of almost 200 fourteen-year-olds. Local residents flattened themselves into fences and hedges when they met us and looked genuinely alarmed. As a teacher, you become accustomed to moving in, through and around hundreds of teenagers every day and it becomes entirely normal. I suppose if you're not used to that situation, it must be pretty daunting. Year Nine was on good form, singing songs as we moved along. I could hear tinny notes from Sony Walkmans and great guffaws of laughter from time to time. We arrived at Southfields Tube station and faced the first challenge of the day which was to safely move the students from the platform into the correct train without losing anyone along the way. Mission accomplished, head count completed, and we were on our way.

I was a bit apprehensive about the Tube change we would have to make along the way, but my colleagues reassured me that they had successfully completed this trip many times over the years. I settled down and relaxed. The kids were great and not at all fazed by Tube travel as it was very familiar to them. All was going well until we had to make our first change. One of the tutors had the group ticket that would cover our journeys there and back across London. This made sense and was easier than trying to keep tabs on every kid with an individual ticket. A group ticket had long been the practice and had gone fine in previous years. But this year, the ticket was in the possession of Stan. Stan was an experienced tutor not known for his patience, his flexibility or, indeed, his liking for teenagers. Perhaps not the best man for the job. Stan waved the ticket at the member of staff, strode through the barrier and set off at a pace without a backward glance. "Stan, wait!" The cry went up from one of my colleagues, but Stan had disappeared from sight. The reality dawned on us quickly. Stan was gone, we had 200 students champing at the bit to get to Southend and we didn't have a ticket between us. What on earth would we do? It was time for an emergency team talk and we decided that the best thing to do was throw ourselves on the mercy of the Tube station staff. They proved wonderful and radioed ahead with permission for us to travel across London to Liverpool Street Station sans ticket! We were eventually reunited with Stan. Did we receive a grovelling apology? Did he show concern for our stressful journey? Not a bit of it. Stan was very cross with us for "dawdling" and holding the journey up. We decided, for the sake of entente cordiale, to leave it at that.

We had a fabulous day out. The kids enjoyed themselves and we made it back to school in the evening without mishap. Imagine how this situation might have played out if it were to occur today. Parents and carers would have received texts and calls from offspring, the incident shared in real time on social media and local journalists would have been licking their pencils in anticipation of a juicy story of disaster on the underground. Instead, while we reflected on what happened and considered how it could have been avoided, nobody was punished, and parents and carers were simply pleased that their children had enjoyed a nice day out. Simples!

Othello

I spent six incredibly happy years at Southfields. I was extremely lucky to have such a fabulous bunch of colleagues and to have opportunities to stretch and challenge myself. I held various positions of responsibility, including acting head of sixth form. This turned out to be a brilliant opportunity that really tested me. I had to take on this role quite suddenly when the head of sixth form became ill. I had been deputy head for a couple of years, but this was quite a step up and I relished it. I inherited an experienced team of tutors and, at just twenty-seven, I was much younger than any of them. They were extremely tolerant and patient and allowed me to step up into this role. Given my lack of experience, they could have been difficult, but they weren't. I learned a lot about leading a team, drawing on the experience of the members of that team, but still having my own vision for the sixth form. Because of this experience, I secured the post of head of English and Media at Tamworth Manor High School in Mitcham. I started work there in September 1996.

The previous head of department was a black British woman, a fact that is relevant to my account of what happened. When we met, she told me that she had experienced deeply offensive comments from students and parents on account of her ethnicity. I was shocked that she had effectively been driven out of her job. The head of the school had done her best to be supportive but it had been too much and so she had decided to leave and move to a different school.

My entry into Tamworth Manor was a baptism of fire. If behaviour at Southfields had been challenging at times, Tamworth was in a whole other league. Students thought nothing of using the foulest language in class and the casual 'effing and jeffing' that abounded turned the air blue. I was not going to put up with this in my classroom, in the classrooms of my team or, indeed, anywhere else within our departmental area. You might ask why I didn't apply that principle to the school as a whole, but I was trying to be realistic by focusing on those areas where I might exert influence. Allegedly, there was a whole school policy and there were some really effective and experienced staff, but it essentially felt like a case of every man and woman for themselves; in those circumstances, pragmatism trumped ideals.

I inherited a Year Eleven group that had done diddly squat the previous year. Many coursework folders were empty and those who had pulled a few pieces together had submitted work that was hardly worth the paper it was written on. They tumbled or swaggered into the classroom for our first lesson and that was where the work began. "Ok, everybody. We'll do that again and before you come into my classroom, you'll line up in silence and I'll tell you when you can come in." A roar went up from some of the lads who clearly found this very amusing. The girls looked at me with utter contempt and, so, the lines were drawn. I was certain that it would be my way or no way and gradually they came to understand that. It took weeks with a number of relapses along the way. One day a vicious fight broke out between one of my students and a peer from a different class. Screams from some girls alerted my colleagues and I to the brawl and we dashed out of our classrooms to see one lad smashing the head of another into the wall. Blood glistened in an arc up the walls. This was serious, an ambulance was called, and the injured party was taken away to be treated. We all felt shaky after this and found it difficult to calm our classes down. Teaching at that school, at that point in its development, was hard. Despite the best planning and careful consideration of classroom management, every day was stressful, as seething tensions between different groups and individuals could erupt at any time and derail lessons. If you have experienced that, you will know exactly what I am describing, but if you haven't taught youngsters, let me tell you that waiting to start a lesson can often generate the same queasy butterflies you might sense before a race or speaking in public. In most settings, you get used to this stage fright and it goes in time as you get to know the students and the systems that are in place to support behaviour expectations. But, if those systems are missing, that feeling may never entirely leave and therein lies at least one significant reason for the exodus of people from the profession. Living on your nerves is tough on the body and mind.

Year Eleven knew early on that this lady meant business and was not for turning. This extended to the year group as a whole and I made sure that I visited all the classes to introduce myself, explain what would and would not be tolerated, and reassure them that getting the best grades possible would be our shared focus and priority. I repeated these key messages lesson in, lesson out and requested that my team do the same. When progress was made, I shared it with the class. They decided they wanted a chart on the wall showing each student's completed pieces of coursework as they were marked and signed off. I was surprised by the public nature of this, but it worked and kept the group on their toes. I grew very fond of that class perhaps because they had initially been so incredibly challenging.

That year, we studied *Othello*, a Shakespearean play that deals with racial prejudice and sexual jealousy, so there was plenty of material to get discussions going. Year Eleven had sort of studied the play in Year Ten but were clearly suffering from collective amnesia, so it was time for a reboot. I had two versions of *Othello* to show them. I decided to use Trevor Nunn's production starring Willard White as Othello, Imogen Stubbs as Desdemona and Ian McKellen as Iago. That version is not as racy as the Oliver Parker production, which I thought was for the best, because too many raunchy scenes might set the students off and I wasn't sure I could rein them back in enough to get the coursework done and dusted!

I had a video cassette of the film version of the play which I would show on the trusty television on wheels that was wheeled from room to room as teachers needed it. A great whoop went up, as it always did at the prospect of watching something rather than having to read or write. I sent up an agnostic prayer that the video player would work, and we were off. I paused the video frequently to explain language and plot and so that the students could make notes. They grumbled about this at first and wanted to just watch it through, but I stuck to my guns and, after several lessons, we got to the end, they had some half-decent notes, and we were ready to begin the dreaded coursework.

They worked hard on their coursework essays, with some tantrums, essays ripped up or screwed into balls and lobbed into the bin, but they stuck with it and everyone produced an essay. It was quite a landmark, and the students were chuffed with themselves. I told them how proud I was of their work and that I wanted to display it on the classroom display board. I explained that it would be good for the lower years to see just how it should be done. That went down very well, and they were all keen to have their work up on the display board. This was a marked change and one I was very pleased to see. I photocopied their work, displayed everyone's essays on the board and packed my bag of marking to take home for the weekend. I left the video of *Othello* on my desk, tidied up, turned off the lights and headed out to the staff car park.

Monday morning arrived. After a coffee and a natter in the staffroom, I set off for my department area. I entered my classroom and immediately knew something was very wrong. The tape had been pulled out of the video cassette and now hung in crumpled coils from the edge of my desk and chair. I surveyed the room and my stomach tightened as my eyes fell on the area where the students' work was proudly displayed. Scrawled across the coursework in angry, black marker pen were the words "Ni**ers out" and "Black c*nts". I froze. I felt sick and frightened.

What followed is now a bit of a haze, but I remember locking the door so that the students wouldn't have to see this horror and almost running back to the main building to find the head. She was absolutely horrified and immediately came with me to take a look. Together, we surveyed this disgusting handiwork in silence. "Right," she said, "I'm contacting the borough solicitor for advice on this." What came to light was sobering. It transpired that my predecessor had endured a far worse time of it than even she had let on. Several parents had threatened her, and had made no attempt to disguise their identities. The borough solicitor had their names and addresses. CCTV footage showed two individuals on site over the weekend who were identified as belonging to this group of parents. The police were informed, and legal action taken. We surmised that these individuals were trying to target my predecessor again and didn't realise that she had already moved on. This seemed the most likely explanation as mine was the only classroom they visited. It was an ugly business, and I will never forget it.

Into the 'civilised' world

In 1997, I left London for a head of English position at a large comprehensive on the outskirts of Cheltenham. I left behind very dear friends, an important network and a marriage that had ended. My eldest daughter was four years old and the upheaval to her life was huge. My husband was from French-speaking Cameroon and had been raised in a village on the edge of a rainforest by friends of his parents. He came from a family of ten children and his parents were simply not able to provide for them all, so he was sent to live away from his family and was raised in a polygamous family. During our marriage, I spent a lot of time with members of his family who lived in France, Belgium and Sweden.

The first morning break in a new staffroom is always a challenge. You have to figure out where to sit, the pecking order among the established staff and a host of other political minutiae. I was used to this, but I was not prepared for my first break in this new staffroom.

In my new role, I would head up a team of thirteen staff, which was a sizeable step up from my team at Tamworth Manor. I was excited by this and had lots of ideas for the term and year ahead. I was also a Gloucestershire girl, and much of what I encountered in the early weeks and months was familiar and I could have easily slid back into the shire except that I wasn't the person I was when I left in 1985. I had seen other places and experienced other ways of doing things and I liked that. But most importantly, I was a mum, and my daughter was a magical fusion of cultures. I was fiercely proud of her.

The first morning's lessons went well. Compared to my previous schools, I found the students extremely easy to manage and to get on task. In the weeks and months that followed, when staff grumbled about how difficult the students were, I smiled to myself and inwardly shook my head in disbelief, but I understood that it was all relative to your experience of challenging behaviour.

At break, I took my place in the coffee queue. Coffee was served every day by a local lady who was the de facto grandmother to all the staff. She was kindly looking and grey-haired with plenty of banter. She welcomed me that morning as a newcomer to the school.

"So, love, where were you working before?" she asked.

I told her that I had been teaching and living in London.

She wiped down the countertop and leaned in with a slightly conspiratorial air, "Well, I expect you're glad to be here and get away from all those n*g n*gs." She smiled and winked at me.

I felt like someone had just punched me in the stomach. I thought of my in-laws and my friends, but mostly I thought of my little daughter at school just up the road in the local primary school. What the hell had I done and what would her experience be? I dealt with this comment in my own way and suffice to say, she got the message.

I wish I could say that this was an isolated incident, but it wasn't, and I really experienced the ugly underbelly of racism from people who would be quick to defend themselves against accusations of racism. They were racist. When you are the white parent, people often reveal their true selves before they know you have a black partner and a mixed heritage child. That has been my experience in the back of taxis, with colleagues, with parents of children I have taught and with people who you would never expect to utter such offensive cra*.

One of my first classes that year was a pleasant enough Year Twelve group. Some of the lads weren't particularly motivated and the girls were noticeably quiet and passive, so getting any kind of discussion going was pretty challenging. But I stuck with it and they loosened up and we had some decent exchanges over the weeks. They all lived locally, and I bumped into students from time to time when collecting my daughter from after-school club. I remember one afternoon walking back to the car, hand in hand with my daughter, talking to her about what she had made at school. Like most four-year-olds, she was very animated and we were deep in conversation.

I heard a familiar voice say, "Alright, Miss."

I turned and saw one of the lads, who I'll call Ben, from my Year Twelve class. "Hello Ben."

"Is that your daughter, Miss?" he asked.

"Yes, it is," I smiled.

He smiled and we went our separate ways.

The following week, I arrived in class to teach Ben's Year Twelve group. When I entered the classroom, the girls looked everywhere but at me, and Ben had a triumphant look on his face. I knew something was wrong, but what? And then I spotted the whiteboard. Written across it was, "Mrs Aitkins likes a bit of black."

Beige

The head of sixth form was something of a legend. Naturally witty and warm, John was adored by the students and universally liked and respected by the staff. Of all the heads of sixth form I've worked with over the years, he remains one of the best I have known. The assemblies he led were always extremely entertaining. To the uninitiated, they often seemed rambling and they were deceptive in their apparent light-heartedness. I was not a sixth form tutor, but if I ever got the chance to attend one of his assemblies, I would make a point of doing so. I attended one assembly where his topic was safe driving. Now, as anyone who has ever learned to drive, tried to teach a teenager to drive or seen reckless behaviour on our roads will know, there are some folks who are immune to advice on this subject. And so it was with many of the sixth formers who sat looking resigned rather than rapt.

John's assembly began with the usual sensible advice about adhering to speed limits, never drinking and driving or getting into a car with someone who has and a host of other perfectly reasonable nuggets of advice. He talked about how to avoid having to collect your car after it's been crushed into a lump of metal that would fit into a carrier bag. This set off a ripple of laughter. Timing was everything with John. He then embarked on one of his eagerly anticipated winding anecdotes that always ended with a great punchline. He described a pupil he had taught and mentored in the sixth form some years before. He described how elated this young man had been when he passed his test and how he had sat in one of John's road safety assemblies "just like you lot are this morning". There were smiles and some laughter. "One morning I had a call from that young man's parents. They needed me to be a character witness for him. He was driving towards a crossroads and thought he would be ok and just carry on. The other car and driver stood no chance." John paused long enough for the horrible realisation to sink in. There was no grinning or giggling now. "I went to court and talked about what a good student he'd been and what a decent individual. I did my best for him, but I couldn't change the facts of what he had done." We were all shocked and the feeling was palpable. I hope now, as I did then, that everyone in that hall that morning, took note of John's story and that it made some difference to how they behaved behind the wheel. I have never forgotten that assembly back in 1998.

I wanted to tell that assembly story to give you a sense of what John was about. He was always lively, inquisitive and lots of fun, but also capable of deadly seriousness when it was needed. Such characters are essential in schools and the fact that he was often instinctive, anti-establishment and had boundless enthusiasm for his subject and his role made him inspiring. There are many such figures in public service, but they are not always thanked for it and, certainly, as time went on and I saw the change and fragmentation from local authority control and the influence of academy chains and MATs, it struck me that the time for mavericks of the best sort was drawing to a close. John would have loathed the new systems and ways and, thank goodness, he didn't have to endure them because there are some people who can never be beige.

And there was certainly nothing beige about John's final assembly which was arranged by the sixth formers. Tutors, students and those of us who had a free period piled in to see John off. We anticipated a review and some good-humoured teasing.

Tutor groups shared their memories of John amid laughter, nodding and nudging in acknowledgement of those events. It felt good and was just what John deserved. He looked so happy and touched by the effort made and the feeling of being part of a school family. His wife, who also taught at the school, was there too to share the experience.

There was a small parting of the waves of students at the back of the hall and a bit of backward glancing distracted us all. I remember looking back and seeing a female police officer. I don't remember exactly what I thought, but it was probably something along the lines of assuming that it was alcohol-related behaviour on the part of our students. The police officer walked down the aisle between the chairs set out on either side. John was on the stage as guest of honour while representatives of each tutor group presented memories of life in the sixth form. The officer was undeterred and pulled out her truncheon, which seemed a tad overzealous. By now we were all a bit confused, with staff and some students looking twitchy. What on earth was going on?

"Is there a Mr John X in the hall?" the police officer called out.

Some of us had that sickening suspicion of where this was going. John said nothing, but some of the students helpfully pointed him out.

The police officer sashayed onto the stage and stood in front of John. "I hear you have been a very bad boy."

The whole episode was horrible. It was inappropriate, utterly humiliating for both parties and badly misjudged by the students responsible. There was an uproar and those responsible for organising it were soon in no doubt that they had horribly misjudged the situation and had committed a serious faux pas.

John was a total gentleman. He took off his jacket and placed it over the young lady's half-naked form. His wife looked stunned, and we all just wanted the floor to open up. Why do I share this memory? Because it illustrates how when working with young people, they can think the world of you but also crush that world like a discarded can of Coke underfoot. It's not personal, it's just growing up.

Something missing

I spent six years at Cleeve School in Cheltenham and went through some significant personal changes. I met a new partner, married again and gave birth to my second daughter. When I read that back now, I wonder where I got the energy to do it all while working. But, of course, I had youth on my side!

As you will have gathered, I have always had a low boredom threshold and a restlessness that has resulted in me needing to seek out change when it doesn't come knocking. The department I led had delivered excellent results, was established and very capable and I felt that my work on this stage of its journey was done. So, what next? Senior management, as it was then called, didn't appeal to me at all and I couldn't see myself in that role. However, I didn't just want to carry on doing what I was doing and I longed for some excitement, some different challenges and to be tested in new ways. I missed working in more urban settings and the opportunities and challenges that went with that. I was extremely fortunate to have the opportunity to qualify as an Advanced Skills Teacher or AST as they were known…well, there were other, less complimentary terms too, but I will leave those to your imagination.

Once I decided on the AST route, there was no stopping me. The head was sceptical but agreed to allow me to apply. I stressed that the outreach element of the role was critical to my decision and I asked for his assurance that this would be honoured. He agreed, but clearly wasn't thrilled. As an AST, it was expected that 20% of my time would be given to outreach. This usually meant working to support colleagues and students in other schools and settings. Some local authorities bore the cost of AST salaries or at least the outreach element of those, so were able to call the tune on that. Years later, as a head teacher myself, the irony of a school losing the input of some of its best teachers while they delivered outreach was not lost on me, but the advantages far outweighed any losses, and it was a fantastic way for a school to retain its best practitioners. In my opinion, the demise of the AST scheme was a real error and the new role of lead practitioner has not had the same credibility because of the ad hoc, in-house assessment process which lacks the rigour of AST application and assessment by an external assessor.

I started my role as an AST and undertook several outreach projects. The most significant of these led me in a direction I could not have anticipated. In the spring term of 2003, I supported colleagues in the English department at Central Technology College in Gloucester. This small, all-boys' school was a secondary modern in nature if not in name, thanks to the ridiculous situation of having four grammar schools in a tiny city. I spent one afternoon a week working with a group of boys considered to be the most able in their year group. My brief was to try and boost their GCSE English Literature grades and their brief was to do all that they could to prevent that! So, it wasn't exactly a meeting of minds. I remember our first lessons clearly. Their behaviour was appalling but not unfamiliar, and I recalled Ursula, the day of The Great Egg Race, crazy moments at Southfields, my Year Eleven class at Tamworth Manor, and the shocking attitudes at Cleeve. But, like a knight, I had won my spurs and I would not be daunted, no matter how hard they tried. Reader, they tried hard!

There is a lot of current discussion, and rightly so, about girls and women constantly running the gauntlet of leering men just to go to the shops, exercise, wear what they want, feel happy in their skin, take a shortcut through a park...the list goes on. When I entered that classroom of Year Ten boys for the first time, my heart rate increased and, in the fraction of a second that it took to read the room, I knew I had walked into a minefield. The question was not if, but when, it would go off.

The class started reasonably well. I explained who I was, what we were going to work on together and what they could potentially achieve. I asked each of them what grade they were hoping for and then made a point of being encouraging but realistic. I was not here to patronise or sell false hope. They were very far behind, would need to work hard and would need to start right now. I asked them if they were willing. I went around the group and, to their credit, they were honest about being lazy, switched off or just a bit lost. As I got to the last three students, the gauntlet was thrown down.

"Miss, can I ask you a question?" asked a student who had been tipping on his chair throughout the discussion. He had smirked at some of the more open responses from his peers and seemed amused by their vulnerability.

"Yes, of course. Fire away."

I won't repeat what he said but suffice to say it was meant to shock and demean and referred to a sexual act in the crudest way possible.

He looked triumphantly around at his peers. Some of them sniggered, while others looked at the floor.

I looked him straight in the eye and said, "I have no idea why you think that it is ok to speak to me like that. I am here to help you and I'm not here to put up with that sort of rubbish. Get out and I will speak to you later when you've had time to think."

He looked around for support from his peers and found that it was not forthcoming. He left the room, slamming the door as he went. Point made. I reported this incident to the head of department, who took it very seriously. The student was sanctioned under the behaviour policy and made to apologise. It proved to be a watershed of sorts and I never encountered behaviour like that from that group again, but what a terrible state of affairs that a student felt emboldened enough to speak that way. I got the distinct impression he was used to throwing his weight around and wasn't expecting to be challenged. He thought wrong.

It may seem rather crude but, in my experience, there often comes a point with a class or an individual, when you must assert your dominance. Being a female teacher in an all-boys' school presented particular challenges and this was just one of several such incidents. But, after my experiences of being both a student and a teacher in all-girls' schools, I was also under no illusion about the equally challenging behaviour of girls. Over the years, I came to realise that I could have words with a male student and really give him a round telling off without any lasting damage to our relationship, while female students would often hold onto a resentment for weeks or even months. Not only that, but their friends would consider you persona non grata as well, even if you had never had a cross word with them. You might think this is a sweeping generalisation, but I base it on three decades of experience. What is also true, in my experience, is that once gained, the respect and loyalty of both male and female students is strong and enduring.

Per ardua ad astra

Over the weeks and months that I supported the Year Ten group at Central, I could feel myself falling in love with the school. I looked forward to my sessions and found myself bored and restless at Cleeve. I was under no illusions about the challenges, and life at Cleeve was undoubtedly calmer and more orderly, but I craved something else and Central was the thing that I craved.

One afternoon, towards the end of a lesson, the head of Central popped in to see me. She sat at the side of the classroom and watched what we were doing. At the end of the session, the boys tucked their chairs under their desks and stood behind them in silence. I then calmly dismissed them. This had taken weeks to accomplish and, on the surface, may sound draconian, but it meant that the boys could ask any questions they needed to before leaving, without having to do so over the din of their classmates, as had previously been the case. It also meant they left in an orderly manner, ready for their next lesson. This worked well for both the naturally loud and gregarious and for the quiet and introverted. That's what good classroom management should be about, promoting the optimum learning environment for all. The head and I spoke about the lesson, the group and some of its characters. She went away seemingly happy with what she had seen and heard.

About two weeks later she approached me and asked if I would consider a full-time post. I didn't need to be asked twice and was delighted at the prospect. A post was advertised; I applied and was interviewed along with the only other candidate who had applied. Central had a dreadful reputation locally and didn't attract many teachers. When I was offered the job, I was over the moon.

I told the head at Cleeve that I would be moving on and I remember him looking at me almost pityingly as he asked, "What on earth do you want to work there for?"

I answered without hesitation, "Because I will make a difference and have a voice."

He was very gracious and said, "Well, if you're sure. I wish you luck and I think you'll be a star."

He and I had crossed swords on several occasions and were not exactly each other's biggest fans, so I appreciated his generous statement.

In September 2003, I joined the staff at Central as a full-time AST and whole school teaching and learning coach. I quickly learned that my enthusiasm and passion for teaching and learning were not universally shared and that my exuberance was not so much grist to the mill as sand in the oyster, but without the resulting pearl! My first INSET (in service training) session centred around the importance of curiosity. I prepared various resources including one that I hoped would go down well and entertain my colleagues. I challenged the staff to a 'taste test' but the titbit to be sampled was, apparently, cat food in a sachet. In reality, it was a washed and cleaned empty sachet of cat food filled with small slices of Mars Bar and lemon jelly. The combined visual effect was of cat food, and it looked very realistic. The session went well and there was plenty of laughter when one brave soul volunteered to eat the cat food and even more laughter when the real contents were revealed. My approach to INSET sessions probably had more to do with my own low tolerance for being talked at for long periods of time and I always blended talking and presentation with activities, something surprising or unusual, if possible, by way of stimulus and plenty of opportunities for questions, observations and cross-group discussions. I was an avid player of bullshi* bingo during INSET sessions run by colleagues over the years, so I was not insensitive to the fact that training sessions could be mind-crushingly boring. I kept a keen eye on my audience for any signs of bullshi* bingo in play!

After a few days at Central, the full reality of the challenges ahead had begun to sink in, and I knew that there would be no easy fixes. I was frustrated by the attitudes of some colleagues who seemed determined to either perpetuate the status quo and ensure that nothing improved or actively block any attempts to put in place systems and structures that might help. I battled with my own classes and had to fight hard to achieve order and make some progress. The Year Ten and Eleven classes were the most difficult as they were used to not being challenged, had exceptionally low expectations of themselves and of me and were open about the fact that they could not wait to leave school. It felt like every man and woman for themselves and just getting through each lesson without a major disaster was an achievement. While this was tiring and, at times, quite frightening, I didn't regret my decision to move to Central and had a stronger sense of purpose than I had felt in a long time. I liked my English department colleagues and enjoyed a shared humour that made the trip to the staffroom worthwhile. We all saw it as a place of refuge and a much-needed oasis.

One morning break, not long after I started at Central, Robin, one of my English department colleagues, came into the staffroom looking incredibly angry. He was sweating profusely and was clearly terribly upset. All eyes turned to him, a mug of coffee was placed in his trembling hands, and we waited to hear what had happened. "I just don't bloody believe them," he said. "I thought I had seen it all and then this." And so began his tale. There was a stock cupboard at the back of each classroom. Robin had gone into his to get some supplies and, while he was in there, the boys had stealthily piled the chairs up into multiple jaunty and perilous Towers of Pisa. Robin was blissfully unaware of what was unfolding until he emerged from the cupboard with spare exercise books. He yelled at the boys to take the chairs down immediately. They took him at his word and kicked the perilously stacked towers so that each crashed to the floor, scattering in all directions. The boys found this highly amusing. Robin did not. It had taken a good ten minutes to get the classroom rearranged and the boys calmed down. I sensed that Robin was in no mood for helpful suggestions about how this might have been avoided, so I kept my thoughts to myself.

Some weeks later, it was my turn to tell a tale in the staffroom and, unfortunately, mine was rather more serious. My Year Ten group was proving particularly challenging. They were a large group of thirty-four students that only just fitted in the classroom. They were obsessed with mother cussing and came up with ever more ingenious ways of insulting each other's mums, leading to absolute mayhem. It was a particularly unpleasant feature of school culture at that time and, as a female member of staff, I found it distasteful, disrespectful to women and a thorough nuisance. One student came up with a highly effective strategy whereby he would write "your mum" on the back of his hand, flash it at one of his classmates and then grin at them or mouth something offensive by way of a sentence finisher. It took me a while to work out what was going on, as often the first I knew of it was when one of the boys shouted across the classroom in anger at the silent insult. Eventually, I worked it out and dealt with the culprit but not before he had managed to cause a serious and dangerous reaction to his mother cussing.

On the occasion in question, the boy flashed his hand with the customary "your mum" on the back. But this time, he picked the wrong boy. Without any warning, both boys were out of their seats and facing up to each other. At that point, I had no idea what had provoked the reaction, but I knew that the situation was becoming dangerously heated. I sent another boy to fetch help. He looked reluctant to do so, sensing he was about to miss something exciting. However, something in the tone of my voice persuaded him and off he went to fetch the member of staff on patrol duty. What happened next is something I will never forget. I can still see it in my mind's eye as if in slow motion. The tussling between the boys became a full-on fight and, before any of us knew it, one boy threw the other hard into the floor-to-ceiling window. He went straight through the glass which shattered into huge, jagged shards. Thank God we were on the ground floor and, by some miracle, he received only superficial cuts. It was a very shocking incident and the entire class stared on in silence. I rushed to the window to check on the boy who had gone flying through the glass and quickly established that he was ok. Help arrived and the two boys were removed, one taken to the first-aid room to be thoroughly checked over and the other to the head's office. Both received appropriate sanctions for their relative parts in this incident and, suffice to say, mother cussing stopped in that class.

Esse quam videri

It was clear that, for the sake of both students and staff, things had to change at Central. However, while it was obvious that the school was in a downward spiral, not everyone wanted to work towards improving it. As I have already mentioned, and as I have come across many times over, a minority of teachers are drawn to schools in crisis because where expectations are low, the pressure is off. Too often I heard colleagues say, "What do you expect? These kids come from…" and the name of a local suburb would be named. I always bristled at this and never let these comments go. That didn't make me popular, but it certainly got the debate going and challenged some of the prejudice and lazy thinking. I must stress that these views were held by the minority and there were many committed and highly dedicated staff at Central. Indeed, I remain in close contact with many of them to this very day and count them as friends rather than simply former colleagues.

Central was a single-sex school and there was an equivalent school for girls. Gloucester has a well-established Muslim community and many parents preferred the single-sex option for their daughters. The only other way to secure single-sex education in Gloucester was to be awarded a place at one of the two girls' or two boys' grammar schools in the town. This was, and continues to be, a rather peculiar feature of this very small city and the resulting impact on the remaining 'comprehensive' schools was that several were, to all intents and purposes, secondary modern schools and not really comprehensives at all. The problem with that was that the ability range was narrow and weighted heavily at the lower end but because the school was described as a comprehensive, the expectations were unrealistic and such schools could never compete fairly against schools with the full ability range. Any attempt to merge Central with the girls' school was fiercely opposed by any number of groups and at least one local celebrity. The proposal was eventually abandoned, and money put aside by Gloucestershire County Council to provide Central with a strategic improvement partner and for the girls' school to receive equivalent funding for its own improvement plans. The only question was, who could take on the challenge and make a success out of Central so that it could once more hold its head high as it had done many years ago? Who could breathe life back into the school's motto, *Esse quam videri*?

The search was on, and a number of well-known organisations applied for the contract. It was an interesting process as each bidder presented what they could offer and what they aimed to achieve if given the opportunity to work with us. By chance, I met a well-respected adviser while at a training session and he recommended Sir Dexter Hutt and the Ninestiles Federation which had a proven track record working with challenging schools in Birmingham. Ninestiles school was the original school and the federation built up around it. I mentioned this to the head, and she made contact with Dexter. The rest, as the saying goes, is history, and the bid submitted by Ninestiles was successful. So began what was later to be described as "a remarkable journey".

A remarkable journey

In October 2005, Ninestiles staff came on their recce and spent several hours walking the school, observing behaviour at crossover times and during break and lunchtime. With a wealth of experience, they knew what they were looking for and Central did not disappoint. Behaviour was atrocious, staff were passive and timid or shouty and aggressive when tackling what was going on. Although we all knew that our visitors were not here expecting to see anything better, our pride did take a bit of a kicking that day. Our visitors were polite and professional throughout the visit, but it was pretty clear what they thought.

Work began in earnest in January 2006 and to say we hit the ground running would be an understatement. I have never experienced anything like the pace at which the Ninestiles staff worked to improve every aspect of the school. Their focus was relentless. Behaviour was tackled in a strategic and carefully planned way. There were detailed surveys of staff and students to get under the skin of which behaviours were holding the school back. The surveys threw up remarkable similarities between staff and student views and gave us much-needed confidence that the behaviour platform we were co-constructing would be stable and something that we could agree on. Having gone through this process several times over the years with other schools, I have never been disappointed by the mirroring of staff and student views on what the behaviour issues are. Six weeks of training and we were ready to implement our new behaviour policy known as Behaviour For Learning (BFL). This became an extremely popular system all over the country and when applied consistently, it works brilliantly.

The curriculum wasn't fit for purpose and, like turkeys lighting their own ovens, Year Eleven were set up to fail as, despite my efforts, many of the options they had chosen in Year Nine meant they couldn't possibly achieve the critical measure of five or more passes at C grade or above. Teaching and learning were woefully out of date and staff had extraordinarily few opportunities for quality INSET or external training. My own efforts as an AST only scratched the surface and I had neither the experience nor the clout to tackle a whole school culture of underachievement. In 2004, I had been appointed curriculum deputy and had started to make some changes to address options but had not been brave or confident enough to make the wholesale changes that were required. Like the rest of my colleagues in the senior team, my days were typically spent firefighting and the focus was on behaviour rather than getting anywhere close to improving teaching and learning, let alone the curriculum. I felt ashamed to call myself a curriculum deputy.

School improvement is an exhilarating business, but it comes with plenty of painful realisations and difficult conversations, often with oneself! One of the first things I was asked by colleagues from Ninestiles was who were the 'big hitters' in terms of behaviour issues and, of those, which boys had the most influence over their peers. Similarly, I was asked which members of staff could be categorised as 'won't' rather than 'can't' when it came to improving their own practice and engaging with improving the school. Based on my experience of the staff and discussions with my senior team colleagues, I named seven staff who fell into the 'won't' camp. I can imagine that some of you are already balking at this idea. You may be thinking, what right did she have to categorise staff in that way and what were their rights in this? These were questions I asked myself too. First and foremost, my belief was, and continues to be, that schools were created to educate and support the development of children. Teachers who do not share that belief are in the wrong profession. You may or may not be surprised to learn that this belief has not always gone down well with colleagues.

With the 'big hitters' established and the 'won'ts' agreed, the next step was to rapidly tackle both problems. Meetings were arranged for each individual 'big hitter' and his parents or carers, we discussed their behaviour records, and we agreed on plans that involved a range of approaches, including managed moves to other schools on a trial basis and permanent exclusion for the seven most disruptive and aggressive students. Again, some of you will be shocked by this. But we were trying to establish a safe and orderly behaviour base in a school that had gone into free fall, and there were some students and their parents or carers who were not prepared to support that. And that was incompatible with our goals. Schools are under tremendous pressure to bend over backwards and accommodate every type of unreasonable behaviour and many heads have lost the confidence to say to parents and carers, enough is enough. While I believe in inclusion, I do not believe in collusion.

The 'won't' staff were also met with individually and a range of ways forward were discussed. Some wanted to move on and were given interview practice and it was agreed that they would receive references stating that their issues were more to do with mismatch than incompetence. Early retirement deals were brokered for several colleagues, and they benefitted from generous deals. We worked with all seven to move on or out in a dignified way, although this process was not without its difficult moments. We worked with regional union reps and, while they fought hard for their members as one would expect, they were also perfectly reasonable, and I never experienced any animosity from them. I was led through this process by Ninestiles colleagues, and it was a masterclass that I will never forget.

One meeting will stay with me forever. It had come to my attention that a member of staff had earned quite the reputation for being 'handy' and I am not referring to his practical skills. Unfortunately, his behaviour management involved being physically aggressive and, once this came to light, it had to be tackled. My mentor and I read through his file right back to the beginning. We both saw a clear pattern of complaints from boys about being pushed against the classroom door or forcibly shoved into the wall. There were several cases of students who had "tripped over and fallen". Neither of us believed that these accounts were true and we had to get to the bottom of it. I felt sickened and angry that too many blind eyes had been turned for so long. We arranged a meeting with the member of staff in question to talk through the content of his file and to ask for his account of these incidents.

My mentor told me to watch and listen but leave the talking to him. I was there to learn and I certainly did not have the experience to lead on such a tricky case. We sat down and the discussion began. The member of staff was on edge, and it was hard to tell whether he was nervous because he was unaccustomed to straight talking or because he felt guilty. The discussion began gently with an invitation to reflect on his years as a teacher, how he felt about being in the profession and the challenges of the job. He started to relax then and opened up about how the boys were so unruly, it was a wonder any of them achieved anything. He told us how little could realistically be expected of boys from "these parts of Gloucester". He was, to coin a phrase, the proverbial turkey lighting his own oven. There was a pause. My colleague leaned forward in his chair, pushed his glasses down his nose and looked over the top of them.

"Thank you for being so candid," he said. "I think I have a better understanding of things now, but there is just something still troubling me which you might be able to help me with?"

I held my breath. Where was this going? The member of staff looked surprised and uncertainty flashed across his face.

"I'll help if I can," he said. "Fire away."

Deadly calm, my colleague went on, "The thing is, I've been working in schools for over thirty years and no pupil has ever tripped over my foot and, yet, I see from your file, that this has happened several times. Could you explain how that happened?"

I hardly dared breathe. Oh my God, did he actually ask him that? What on earth would he say? I worked hard at maintaining as neutral an expression as I could muster. The member of staff started to splutter in anger. What was interesting though was he didn't deny these "trips and falls" and his indignation sounded hollow. He knew he had been rumbled. What followed was a swift resolution. Arrangements were made for a meeting with a union rep to agree next steps. What wasn't an option was remaining in this school or, indeed, any other. His dislike of youngsters, his contempt for those he saw as somehow unworthy of his time and his toxic attitude towards the ethos we were trying to create meant that it was time for him to go. He received a decent financial settlement and was able to move on to pursue a job he was better suited to. I learned a lot from that meeting and reflected on it many times over the years. I came across several staff over the years who were simply not suited to the profession and, while those conversations were never easy, I vowed I would never turn a blind eye.

The transformation of the school was a complex and delicate process. HR or discipline matters involving students can be long-drawn-out and fraught. I was both fortunate and unfortunate to have the support that I did to undertake these challenges – fortunate because we moved mountains swiftly and unfortunate because it created an expectation that such matters could always be dealt with swiftly. In reality, that was generally not the case. Being part of a hard federation where accountability for every aspect of school performance was shouldered by Ninestiles meant that I could learn and take risks with the considerable protection of a host of highly experienced colleagues. How would I have fared as a lone deputy in a failing school without that? I can hazard a guess!

An accidental headship begins

It was 20 February 2006, my youngest daughter's fourth birthday. But I was not to spend much of it with her. The head teacher had become unwell and, as the only deputy in the village, so to speak, I was asked to act up. So began a period of my life that daily called upon me to make choices between work and family. All working parents well know the swings between guilt and exhilaration, but I had no idea what I was embarking upon, which was probably for the best. I remember giving my daughter an extra tight squeeze, wishing her a happy birthday and kissing her goodbye as I mentally juggled the day ahead. My elder daughter was approaching thirteen and very much in need of my full focus and, yet, I chose to step onto a steeper professional path and did so, if not blindly, then at least with little idea of what lay ahead. We three have talked many times over the years about our individual and collective experiences of that very prickly meshing of my home and work life.

I arrived at work with a tatty bouquet of flowers that I had bought at the garage en route. My PA found me a vase to deposit them in and I sat in the head's chair. I had never had a PA before and was not at all sure what was expected. I swivelled around and around in the chair like a child and couldn't help feeling excited. What would this be like?

I had never planned to be a teacher, let alone a head teacher and the chair of governors had already raised a question about my gravitas. This was an accidental headship for sure but, nevertheless, it was a role I was keen to try. What I remember of that first day is a constant rise and fall of confidence which led me to make decisions and then be plunged into doubt about those same decisions. Should I just press on and show everyone I could take the helm or was it better to check in with colleagues on every key decision? Of course, there is no right answer, so I plumped for the middle ground and, over the weeks, found a groove that kept me from making really stupid decisions, but one which did not slow the much-needed pace of change required. I shall forever be indebted to my executive head and mentor, Sir Dexter Hutt, and my chair of governors, Vanessa Aris, MBE, who helped me so much in those early days and weeks.

Three weeks into the headship I received the dreaded call from Ofsted. The woman on the other end of the line must have thought I had lost the plot, as my first response was, "No, you're not supposed to come yet." As Cnut had discovered before me, there are some tides you simply cannot hold back. When the inspection happened, I experienced moments of real frustration and a sense of unfairness at the criticisms that rained down thick and fast fell on my burning ears. Inwardly, I was chuntering, but I learned an important lesson that day, one that was pushed home to me by Dexter. He pointed out that accepting the role of acting head a) was not a matter of 'acting', it was very real and b) with the role and title came accountability so, whether I felt it was fair or not, I had to take the feedback, digest the uncomfortable truths and get on with the job in hand. The job in hand was to shift Central rapidly from a school issued with a 'notice to improve' to being a 'good' school.

Every cup has a furry lining

One of the significant strengths of Central, even when it was struggling, was the very considerable warmth and good humour of the staff. They loved to tease each other and there was a lot of banter which I thoroughly enjoyed both as a member of the teaching staff and then as the head. An eagerly anticipated event was the annual review, performed each Christmas and featuring sketches that parodied *Dr Who*, *I'm a Celebrity*, *Holby City*, *Little Britain* and many more. The boys absolutely loved it and those of us who performed in it enjoyed much hilarity during rehearsals. One year, I played *Little Britain's* Vicky Pollard and my monologue used her famous "yeah but, no but" and included the names of many of the students and classic Central antics. This went down very well. Another favourite was the take-off of *I'm a Celebrity*, complete with the infamous bush tucker trial which, if you're not familiar with it, involves eating things like locusts, fish eyeballs and so on. We bought edible locusts for the occasion and one of our teaching assistants made a very realistic eyeball out of a small ball of Mozzarella and food colouring. Yes, I know. You are probably thinking, perhaps a little less time larking about and more time focusing on school improvement might have been wise, but what I know of schools is that a staff that laughs together and better still, a staff and student body that laughs together, also works better together.

The fun extended to our assemblies, our charity events, a trip to Bristol Zoo and even flying a plane over Gloucester with a banner proclaiming our first set of half-decent exam results and advertising our school on the back and side of buses using the tag line 'Success in the City' which I sort of pinched from *Sex and the City*. There was something very strange and rather funny about driving behind a bus with my own face smiling back at me. The boys loved to tell me when they'd spotted one of 'our buses'. I had a suspicion that colleagues from nearby schools found our bus campaign deeply irritating. Was that in any way part of the appeal of doing it? I couldn't possibly say. I think we were one of the first schools to do this but certainly not the last. Over the years, I have seen a fair few such advertisements about and have to smile to myself when I remember ours from 2007. We packed a lot into those years but, while laughing, we were also deadly serious about improving our school.

The staffroom, like most staffrooms I have spent time in over the years, had a perennial 'mug problem'. The problem was the selective amnesia that set in when it was someone's turn to wash up their mug after they'd had a break or lunchtime cuppa. We tried rotas, departments taking turns, nagging, leaving the cups to pile up into festering heaps, but nothing worked and it really was becoming an issue. The science department used to joke that the school budget could be helpfully supplemented by sales of penicillin growing in the mugs. Mind you, 'The Independent Republic of Science' didn't like slumming it in the staffroom and stayed in their own departmental area with clean cups and very willing science technicians to keep things tidy. Their prep room area was the envy of the rest of the staff and their Friday team lunches were legendary and a thing to behold. You knew you had really made it in the school pecking order when you were invited to a Friday lunch with the science team.

Mug-gate eventually came to a head and a solution was found in the shape of a dishwasher. It really was that simple. Who knew! Then the battles raged about whose turn it was to load and unload it. As one of my colleagues put it so brilliantly, "At Central, every cup has a furry lining."

Behaviour, behaviour, behaviour

When we first started working together, Dexter asked if I thought we should prioritise teaching and learning or behaviour. As a former AST, I was pretty confident that the answer was teaching and learning. But Dexter shook his head and said no, it was behaviour. I was indignant and waded in to defend my position. Dexter listened and then explained his experience and rationale. Staff and students rely on good behaviour to create the right conditions for undisturbed and safe learning and teaching. While an individual staff member may be able to create a climate conducive to learning in their own classroom through dint of their personality, the relationships they build over time, their talent, and so on, the business of a head and the team is to ensure that everyone has the support of a secure behaviour platform, and this should not be left to individual members of staff. Indeed, the sign of an effective behaviour policy is when it works as well for newly qualified or student teachers as it does for experienced, senior teachers. This was at the heart of BFL and, when used consistently, its power to transform behaviour was truly something to experience. Fundamental to this policy were consequences and sanctions for choices that resulted in lost, disturbed or prevented learning. This was not about discipline and punishment.

The pastoral deputy from Ninestiles was Garry Llewellyn. He was warm and funny, and he loved his job. He was passionate about the power of BFL to transform schools and students' lives. In the early days of our working relationship, when I had recently been appointed acting head, Garry spent two days each week at Central. His presence was invaluable. He was happy to walk the school, meet stroppy students, provide support at parental meetings, and generally help us out and show us the way. He was chirpy, full of jokes and hilarious anecdotes and, when he was on site, you felt like nothing could go wrong. Dexter had the same effect and, between them, they breathed confidence and calm back into the very fabric of the school. Such figures in schools can never be underestimated for the tremendous stability they bring, and we all sighed with relief when they came to work with us. They were both utterly fearless when faced with challenging behaviour from students and, on occasion, parents and carers.

When I became acting head, there was a student in Year Seven who took defiance to a whole new level. He came from a very troubled background and had serious learning difficulties in addition to social and family challenges. The odds were heavily stacked against him, and he came to us with a troubling track record of exclusions. He started off the new academic year on the wrong foot and was exceedingly difficult to settle. He had support from our fabulous Learning Inclusion (LINC) team, headed by Mandy Pugh, who worked wonders with some of our most challenging and needy boys. But each day with this boy brought further incidents and, by the end of the first week, he had already been excluded for punching one of his peers. After several weeks, his attendance became poor and then nosedived. What to do? I sought Garry's advice. We talked through his background, his primary school behaviour report and the incidents logged since he had come to Central. His mum would not engage, and we had already worked out that she had no control over her son.

"Time for a home visit," Garry said, with a twinkle in his eye that grew even more twinkly when he saw the look of consternation on my face.

I had never done a home visit and wasn't too sure what this might entail.

"Get your coat. We'll take the Saab."

With that, we set off into the outskirts of Gloucester with the top down on the car, me wearing Garry's pink scarf for extra warmth and music playing at full volume. The Saab had been Garry's retirement gift to himself when he 'technically' retired that year but, of course, Garry being Garry, he wasn't ready to retire and had bags of energy. In fact, he often had more energy than colleagues half his age!

We pulled up outside the student's home and knocked briskly at the front door.

"Who is it?" a wary voice called out from inside.

We explained who we were and that we were concerned about the boy's absence. Eventually we were invited in. The house was immaculate and mum was very pleasant. She explained that her son was still in bed and would not get up.

"I'll get him up," said Garry. "Leave it with me." With that, he walked to the foot of the stairs and called up, "Hello X, it's Mr Llewellyn here. I'm here with Mrs Anthony. We've come to talk to you and see if we can help you to get back into school."

No answer. We waited.

Then Garry said, "Can you see the car parked outside?"

There was the sound of movement from upstairs and then a mumbled, "Yeah."

"Well, if you are going to come back to school today, you'll probably need a lift so we thought you might like to come back to school with us?"

There was no response and clearly the boy wasn't falling for this blatant bribery...or so we thought. Next came the sound of rustling and footsteps and slowly but surely, he came downstairs wearing jogging bottoms and a T-shirt which suggested that he was not actually planning on returning to school any time soon.

His mum looked at him wearily and said, "You've gotta go back to school. You'll get me in trouble if you don't."

"Shut up!" he scowled at her with contempt.

We both turned to him and said, almost as one, "Don't talk to your mum like that."

"Fuc* off!" he replied, putting us back in our boxes.

With that, he launched himself at the back of the sofa and hung upside down from the back of it with his legs hooked over, swinging like a small, disgruntled fruit bat. I looked at Garry, looked at the boy's mum and then back at the boy. Now what?

Garry settled down into an armchair with his back to the boy and, with an apparent nonchalance that must have taken superb acting skill, struck up a conversation with the mum, all the while ignoring the taunts and expletives emanating from the back of the sofa. They talked about family, problems with the neighbours, what the boy was like when he was little and so on. Eventually the swinging stopped and so did the expletives. It was time to try again.

"Well, X, what do you think about coming back to school with us now?"

He paused and marshalled his finest verbal weaponry. "Fuc* off, you old, bald-headed pric*!"

I took a sharp intake of breath. What on earth would Garry say to that? Surely, he would be angry?

Garry turned to the boy and, with almost Churchillian sangfroid, said, "I say, less of the old."

I had to smother a giggle. The boy looked decidedly fed up that his 'bomb' had been so efficiently diffused. Somehow the fight went out of him and, with a bit of grumbling, he reluctantly went upstairs to put on his uniform. When we got in the car, Garry put the roof down, and the boy was allowed to sit in the back where he would get the full open-top car experience! What a strange sight we must have been; Garry at the wheel of a super, black, shiny Saab convertible, me in the front with a baby pink scarf wrapped round my head and neck and the boy in the back making 'gestures' to motorists as we sailed past them. I like to think that was a happy experience for him and that perhaps he remembers it from time to time. Sadly, his path through Central came to an abrupt end and he was permanently excluded before the end of the academic year.

One of my colleagues on the senior team was a very experienced pastoral lead. With the support of Ninestiles colleagues, he led the implementation of BFL. We were trained over six weeks and the entire policy was built around self-identified behaviours that we saw as barriers to teaching and learning. It is worth pointing out that, in this sense, BFL is very much bespoke to each school and is not, as detractors have claimed, either a 'one size fits all' approach or a system that deskills staff. What it did and does is focus the scrutinised collective energy of staff to work as a team to challenge and eradicate non-learning behaviours and to encourage and reward positive learning behaviours. It eliminated the need for staff to spend breaktimes and lunchtimes setting and supervising their own detentions and, instead, they worked as a team to supervise whole school detentions approximately once every six weeks. This also removed the problem of students choosing which detentions they would attend based on their own 'hierarchy of authority'.

Central's behaviour had been appalling and, at times, dangerous. BFL created safe and orderly corridors, gave teachers a fighting chance of starting each lesson briskly and delivering what they planned to deliver, and it significantly increased what could be covered in each lesson. The latter came as quite a shock and, in the early days of BFL, staff ran out of material to teach because they had been so used to losing 50% or more of teaching time due to poor behaviour and inattention. Having to plan more was a nice problem and one of the signs of the green shoots of improvement that we were all desperate to see.

We worked hard on BFL and, at the end of each of the first few weeks of implementation, we scrutinised the data to see what patterns were emerging and how to address them. After the first half term, all staff members had an opportunity to talk about the sanctions they had issued, support they needed and students they had identified as particularly challenging. It certainly wasn't plain sailing once BFL was in place. But we had created high expectations, provided support for those staff and students who needed it and maintained a relentless focus on getting it right. Assemblies, which had been like crowd control at best and bedlam at worst, became a pleasure and we were able to take greater risks because we now had a structure in place. We did things such as getting the whole school to participate in a Mexican wave, ran karaoke assemblies, had a rowing demonstration, and a particularly brave assembly about testicular cancer delivered by one of my deputies which began with an image of male genitals projected onto the huge projector screen. Assemblies offered an opportunity to come together as a whole school, remind everyone of our values and core purpose, learn something new, laugh and enjoy each other's company, but also reflect on individual and school challenges.

In May 2007, we were reinspected by Ofsted. The lead inspector and his colleagues investigated every aspect of the school and were keenly interested to see what improvements had been made since the disastrous inspection of the previous year. We were absolutely over the moon to be graded as 'good' and named the most improved school in the southern region. The report read beautifully and described our year of graft as being a "remarkable journey" and how students talked with "glee" about the improvements to their school. Reading those two comments was pure magic. As it turned out, the report was not the end of the connection, as the lead inspector contacted me the following year and invited my pastoral deputy, Martin, and I to undertake some work in Bahrain. On a misty, cold November evening in 2008, we flew out to Bahrain for another, remarkable journey.

How big is yours?

Martin and I landed in shimmering heat and glorious sunshine. The contrast with the dismal November gloom we had left was enough to get the adrenaline coursing for the few days we spent in Bahrain. We were driven to our hotel and, having checked in, were collected by our host and the former lead inspector. During our visit we trained ministers, government officials and teachers from a range of schools on the development and implementation of BFL. Several teachers talked openly about poor behaviour and how difficult it was to sanction, as parents and carers would not support what they saw as punishment. We talked through one of the underlying principles of BFL which is that all actions have consequences, which can be positive or negative. We explained that students have the choice to behave badly or well but there must be clear consequences for those choices and issuing those consequences needed to be consistent across the school. The ministers and officials listened politely and asked reasonable questions, but I couldn't sense whether they would follow up with decisions and policy. The teachers, on the other hand, would have started there and then if given the chance and it was clear that they were desperate for change and support.

Over coffee, we met a couple of the head teachers. Martin and I had clearly been introduced as deputy head and head teacher, respectively, of Central Technology College, but this was apparently trumped by a cultural filter which, when looked through, reversed our positions.

A gentleman in dishdash approached us. He struck quite an impressive figure. I had only ever seen such clothing on television or in films, so to be standing for the first time among men dressed in this way was quite something. The man turned to Martin and introduced himself as head of the school that was hosting the training conference that day.

"So, you are headmaster," he said. "It is very good to meet you." He nodded at Martin and offered a bonding type of smile.

"No, I'm not the head teacher. Helen is," Martin replied, as he stepped back a little to emphasise the point.

Normally, we operated in a non-hierarchical way and were simply a team, but Martin quite rightly recognised that this was an issue. I will always remember his sensitivity and wisdom that day.

The head teacher turned to me and, with a withering look and barely concealed disbelief, said, "You are headmaster of a boys' school? In my country, that would never be allowed."

I drew myself up to my full five feet two inches, adjusted the head covering that was slipping off my head and looked him straight in the eye. "I am the head teacher and, in England, it is perfectly common to have female head teachers of all-boys' schools." I had no idea what the actual statistics were and I didn't actually know any other female heads of boys' schools, but I knew there must be some out there and, in any case, I was feeling pretty rattled now.

He looked at me again with a mixture of what can only be described as pity and contempt and came in for his final flourish. "My school has 1,000 boys. How many boys do you have?"

He'd got me there, but I was in the ring now, so I responded, "I have 430." Do not forget the all-important thirty!

This seemed to please him no end and, with a triumphant toss of his head, he cried, "Hah, mine is bigger than yours!" With that, he bustled off in a swish of robes and self-importance.

Martin and I chuckled about this in the car on the way back to the hotel.

"Bloody cheek of him. How dare he assume I'm not the head just because I am a woman."

"I've never seen you look so pissed off," Martin laughed. "I thought you were going to deck him."

"Mine is bigger than yours" became a line we trotted out over the years when we thought someone was being an idiot or showing off. It proved useful on more than one occasion!

Exile

One morning we were collected by a colleague who worked as a consultant in Bahrain. He had been there for almost a year, so knew the systems and practices quite well. He was a great companion for the day and filled us in on all sorts of useful and interesting cultural details. He took us to visit a girls' primary school and explained the basic principle behind head teacher placements. Martin and I were pretty gobsmacked to discover that head teachers could be placed in schools and moved on without their agreement. There was a sort of football league of schools and if you failed to perform well in your job or made waves, you were moved to a school lower down the league. Martin and I were both fascinated and horrified by this and talked about it a lot during our visit. We deduced that the system could potentially lead to fear, with schools forever consigned to being led by 'failing heads'. On the other hand, a school might benefit from the unintended consequence of gaining a highly effective head who had been moved because he or she was perceived as bolshie, not toeing the line or other variations on the theme of being a bit of a free spirit. The head we were going to visit definitely fell into the latter camp.

The school was enchanting. The attractive building and site were located towards the south of the island. Inside, the school was immaculate and the classrooms looked full of the busy activity you would hope to see in any good primary school. But this was not regarded as a desirable school and the head, while clearly dedicated and highly effective, had been moved there from her previous, higher-ranking, school for some unspoken crime against the system. We did not ask, and she did not tell. We understood that to try and draw her into such a discussion could be problematic for her and we had no desire to create waves. She had suffered enough already. Despite having had this school forced upon her, it was clear that she had embraced it and was working extremely hard to raise standards and give these little girls the best education she could. Martin and I left that visit feeling impressed and rather humbled by the head and utterly aghast at the system she was doing her best to work within. We came across many inequalities, including different pay grades for staff according to their country of origin and parent 'voice' that made the pushiest parents we encountered at home look like lambs in comparison.

We drove away in pensive mood. We saw the shimmering heat haze which turned the road into a shifting, undulating snake ahead of us. At one point, we slowed to a crawl when we got stuck behind an open-topped truck piled high with animal carcasses. Blood dripped from the truck to the road and left a long trail of bloody artistry like a macabre Jackson Pollock painting. We didn't talk much on the homeward journey as we were both lost in thought. My brain was whirring as I thought about how one might help to bring about change. I wondered how I would have coped working in such a system. I wondered whether Gloucester city and its peculiar grammar and comprehensive school system wasn't in many ways just as bad, with the embedded snobbery and class inequality that such a system perpetuated. This thought depressed me, but I also felt my determination grow to keep pushing the boundaries for Central. The trip to Bahrain was not an epiphany, and I wouldn't be so pretentious to claim it as such, but it certainly gave Martin and I renewed energy and determination to do the absolute best for our boys and staff.

Reality based learning

What sort of learner are you? Do you know? Do you care? Does it matter? As a keen bean studying the craft of teaching during my PGCE, I came across the idea that one might be a visual, aural or kinaesthetic (VAK) learner. During the 1990s, we talked a lot about these different learning styles and many an INSET day began with a quiz to assess which type we were and there were opportunities to explore this with students too. As with all education 'silver bullets', reality wasn't quite so simple. There are many far more qualified than me who can discuss VAK theory, but I know from personal and professional experience that it is unlikely that any of us are simply one type of learner, and context, time of the day, whether there is a wasp or a fart in the classroom, can all have a bearing on how we learn best at any given moment. As a teen, I loved listening to the radio and certain teachers had voices that I could also happily listen to for long stretches, so long as they wove humour and real-life experiences into what they were explaining or describing. When it came to learning a skill, no amount of listening or watching worked as well as being given the chance to be hands-on, to try it out and get it wrong from time to time. Visual learning worked well for me when I watched someone doing what they loved. The common thread wasn't type of learner or preferred learning style, it was the link to learning and authentic experiences.

Ninestiles was a trailblazer for several key approaches and, where Ninestiles went, we followed. Over time, however, that shifted from an apprentice role to developing our own mastery.

Most of us have learned about World War I. We all have more or less detailed knowledge about it, depending on personal curiosity, how we were taught about it at school, our age and other factors. But how many of you have experienced trench foot, cooked in an open trench, or held the very same weapon used by a WWI soldier in your hands? I could be wrong, but I suspect very few. I smile because I know approximately ninety young men who attended a series of special learning sessions at Central in 2008 who did just that.

Along with Martin, my other brilliant deputy at Central was Julian. He was curriculum deputy and a passionate historian. He became a key driver for Reality Based Learning (RBL) at Central and I remain indebted to him for his flair, energy, and sheer bloody-mindedness when it came to making things happen. I was extremely fortunate to have Martin and Julian as my key colleagues. Both were phenomenal powerhouses in their respective areas and there was nothing we three couldn't achieve when we put our collective wills together.

Central had fallen in favour as a local school. Regular pasting by the press, the tragic death of a pupil, an ailing budget and lousy results led to an inevitable and sharp decline in students. When I first arrived at Central as a visiting AST, there were 110 boys in Year Eleven. When I became acting head in September 2006, we welcomed only fifty-six boys into Year Seven. Something had to change and fast.

The changes we made around behaviour were essential to stabilise the school and create confidence. In addition, we recruited new staff, made curriculum changes and did most of the obvious things one does to improve a school. Then, we set about marketing ourselves in earnest. I've already told you about the buses and planes, but what about creating a buzz about teaching and learning and offering something unlike anywhere else? We decided on an annual transition project for all boys who transferred to the school each September.

One day, I heard Martin and Julian guffawing in their office next door to mine. They were up to something. A knock on my door and in they came, looking shifty but triumphant.

"Helen, we've had an idea and you mustn't say no."

I looked at their excited faces. How could I resist…hmm… "Go on then."

"Well, you know we've always fancied making a trench on the field?"

"Um, yes…" I replied.

"Well, Paul (our site manager) says he knows where we can hire a digger to build one and it's available today so we were wondering, can we go and get it?"

Now, you are probably thinking, woah, hang about, what is all this about a trench and a digger? That's come out of nowhere. Well, yes and no. We had talked about creating a replica WWI trench for the boys to experience life in the trenches as part of a history unit. While I had enjoyed the fantasy idea, I hadn't exactly reached the green light stage but, clearly, Martin and Julian had. What was the worst that could happen? Looking back, possibly quite a lot but, on that morning, with my deputies positively radiating energy, I could do nothing but give my blessing and off they went in a flash to pick up the digger!

The digger arrived and Martin, Julian and Paul set to work. The photographs I have from that time still make me smile. Initially the trench was just a small scar in the ground but it quickly grew into a full-scale replica trench. It was kitted out for 'CTC First Battalion' and, when it was complete, it was quite simply amazing. We stood and stared at it and imagined the looks of glee and excitement on the faces of the boys when they saw it for the first time.

With the trench built and dressed, planning continued apace. When the morning came to welcome our new recruits, we were all super excited. The first day of the transition project was brilliant. The boys experienced the closest thing to trench foot as they hobbled around the field wearing socks filled with hair gel and sand; they cooked outside using mess tins and basic fire-lighting equipment and held weapons from WWI and, above all, understood something of the brutality of the experience and how we must endeavour to eradicate war at all costs. We were aware of the inherent dangers of in any way glamorising war and the experience of war, so we emphasised reality and intelligent engagement over fantasy and vicarious thrills. I believe we got the balance right and I am eternally grateful to and appreciative of the work of my Central colleagues who made possible not just that particular five-week project but all the others too. Dexter and colleagues at Ninestiles and Vanessa Aris, our chair of governors, also worked so hard to stabilise the school and create conditions where risk-taking was possible. Without their experience, expertise, and encouragement, much of what I describe about Central would never have happened.

We kept the trench until 2010. At that point, Central was amalgamated with another local school to form an academy. The trench had served us well but had started to deteriorate and had to be filled in. We were incredibly sad about this decision, but it was one of many aspects of the end of the school and the end of an era that we dealt with. As you know, the battlefields where so many lost their lives in France are today marked in vivid red by the poppies that grow there. The symbolism is well known and the science too; turning over of the soil through explosions, gunfire and other turbulent actions stimulated the conditions for poppies to grow. Our trench also delighted us with poppies and, I must confess, we were very moved by this sight and poignantly felt a link to the past.

Maths with a difference

Beware the national strategies, for they have come but not yet passed. I am old enough (good grief) to remember the government's literacy and numeracy strategies. Well meant, undoubtedly; carefully planned, probably; welcomed by those of us 'fortunate' to be chosen to receive them...not so much. Amazing as this may sound, most schools do not particularly enjoy being advised by consultants and I should know, as I have worked as one in the 'autumn' years of my professional life! To paraphrase, it is a truth universally acknowledged that a head teacher in need of advice does not want it if it comes from a consultant. Cue the Teflon-coated approach of the national strategies. These strategies were sensible and you couldn't really argue with them, but they were dull, dull, dull. At Central, we had an almost allergic reaction to 'dull' and yup, that sometimes got us into trouble, got on people's nerves but, my goodness, it served us well as a bullshi* detector.

The strategies came with plenty of money, resources and, if you were lucky, a credible consultant. Ours was ace and had been a highly successful school head in Coventry. Dexter had introduced me to him several years earlier, and we had visited his school. He arrived as a consultant with boxes to tick but left as a friend, confidante and ardent supporter of what we were trying to do.

113

One of the common challenges for those of us in the 'elite club', i.e. national strategies schools, was that, while we could assemble and retain good English departments, half-decent maths teachers were as hard to find as a grounded Kardashian and, believe me, to secure one was as costly, particularly in a school like Central. We were fortunate to have a full 'complement' of maths teachers, but our only option for head of department was super numerate, super bright, but disinclined. This is not an unusual feature of really good teachers who like being in the classroom, enjoy teaching kids but don't want to manage their colleagues. The AST scheme was created for this very purpose but, at this point and in this context, we needed a head of maths. The disinclined maths teacher accepted and then I added a new challenge to his plate – head of 'mathemenglish'. This entailed overseeing the progress and tracking of both maths and English, focusing on those students in danger of securing a C in one subject but not the other, reorganising teaching groups, organising skills-focused revision sessions and, above all, keeping the teams talking to each other and sharing the responsibility and the goal of at least 30% of the students achieving five GCSEs at C grade or above, including in maths and English. That might not sound overly ambitious, but for us and for our boys, it was the highway to heaven…or, at least, the highway out of the 'elite club'.

We made it out and were so chuffed with and for our boys. In those days, students could take the exam multiple times and could enter early if they were ready. As someone who had taken their maths O level several times to secure a C, I did, and always will, support the opportunity to retake. In my case, it took one particular teacher to explain maths to me in a certain way for me to see the light. I would never deny that opportunity to others and, in later years, when I moved to Fortismere, when schools came to be judged by 'first sit' results, I took the unpopular decision to continue with early entry and another shot in Year Eleven. The heads of some other schools thought I was stupid. Others opted to do the same.

And, so, to my 'favourite' strategy – the numeracy strategy. How do you get youngsters excited about maths? Hmm…it's an interesting challenge. For one day at least at Central, we cracked it.

Imagine or remember, lessons about plotting coordinates. Super dull. Super irrelevant for most of us. Super necessary to pass maths/geography O levels and an important part of a GCSE. Now, imagine a plane and a chap with a parachute. Imagine you must plot the coordinates for the plane to hover over and the chalk circles on the ground that the chap will aim to land on. Imagine if this was going to actually happen in front of your very eyes.

A whole school assembly was arranged. Martin, Julian and I were there to supervise and support. The hall was packed and the boys in the tiered seating shuffled in their seats in anticipation. At the front of the hall on our legendary big screen, the head of maths gave a masterclass in coordinates. Each tutor group was then invited to submit their estimated coordinates for where the parachutist would land and they were encouraged to consider weather conditions, including wind speed. Once this was done, we waited in eager anticipation until the message came that the plane was overhead. The entire school trooped out onto the school field and we arranged ourselves around the edge of the cordoned-off area in which the coordinates had been drawn on the ground with the paint we used to mark out the racetrack. It was both exciting and nerve-wracking. We craned our necks to catch the first glimpse of the parachute in descent. After circling several times, the small plane reached its optimum position and the parachutist leaped from the plane and began to descend. Students and staff shouted with excitement. Where would he land? Which group had picked the winning coordinates? And, most importantly, would he land safely?

All went smoothly and the parachutist landed on the target with a puff of white paint dust. A huge roar went up and we all clapped until our hands ached. The coordinates were logged, the winning tutor group were told the good news and we got to meet the team involved in the jump. This wonderful experience was made possible by a colleague on my senior team who had pulled some strings with contacts at RAF Brize Norton. They did a wonderful thing for us that day and I know there are former students out there who are now grown men with families who will remember that experience to this very day. How different it would have been to learn about coordinates through a textbook or worksheet. Now, of course one cannot have parachute jumps every day of the week but, for the learning created, the impact and shared community experience, it was and is worth investing in such events and experiences as often as possible, and they do not have to be on such a grand scale to have huge value.

Asylum

Central was becoming an increasingly popular school choice for asylum seekers, who were predominantly from Iraq and Afghanistan. Indeed, in our final year as Central, 14% of the student population was made up of such youngsters. They arrived in and around Gloucester, often offloaded in industrial parks and local car parks like discarded goods. At times, it was shocking and heartbreaking and, as a mother myself, I could only begin to imagine the agony of family members who remained in their home country and who had to say goodbye to their sons, quite possibly without any hope of seeing them again. These boys were often traumatised, not only by the experience of landing in an alien country and culture, but by what they had lived through and witnessed before leaving their home countries. For some, their first day at Central was their first ever day at school. Many did not speak a word of English and had no family members around to offer comfort and guidance through the acute and ongoing anxiety surrounding their status as asylum seekers.

Helping to settle these boys in was a whole school effort, requiring visits to their bed and breakfast accommodation to check its suitability, arranging for new bedding and clothing after one group of boys contracted scabies in their accommodation, trips into Gloucester to practise language skills in real-life scenarios, teaching basic cooking skills so those not placed with foster carers could fend for themselves and, of course, helping them to navigate daily life at school and beyond the school gates. How did the rest of our students respond to these new arrivals? Well, the responses were mixed, as you might imagine. Many of our students were exceedingly kind, taking the new boys under their wing, including them in games of football, inviting them to hang out after school and at weekends and helping them find their way around school and from lesson to lesson. Others were less welcoming and there were some territorial fights between the boys that had to be sorted out and dealt with swiftly and firmly. Fights at Central were exceedingly rare but it became evident that some of our newer boys were quite literally used to fighting for survival and it took some of them months to become less reactive and for the fight, flight, fright response to be calmed. Given what many of them had experienced, this was hardly surprising, so we took an approach of compassion with firm boundaries and insisted on finding non-violent ways to deal with conflict.

We were about two weeks into the settling in period for our latest new arrivals, all from Afghanistan. They were a very mixed group with clear differences in education levels, upbringing, expectations of life in England and understanding of the language. It was important to constantly remind ourselves that while these boys shared a country of origin, a language and a religion, it would be a grave error to treat them as a sort of 'unit' requiring the same approaches. It was second lesson of the day, and I was on patrol call-out. This was a rota staffed by the senior leadership team and involved being on call to help with any behaviour issues that required a student to be removed from his lesson. The patrol phone rang, I answered and was soon on my way over to the PE block. One of our new arrivals was refusing to change into his kit or participate in the lesson. This in itself was unremarkable, as students often accidentally on purpose 'forgot' their kit to dodge PE. What was odd about this situation was that the student in question had been impeccably polite since arriving at Central, could understand most instructions given to him because he spoke reasonable English and, furthermore, had his kit with him. Clearly something else was up, so I decided to take the student to my office to see if he would open up during the walk back across the playground.

I began my questioning in a general and non-accusatory way. "How are you settling in?" I asked.

"Yes, very good, Miss, thank you."

"Is there anything we can do for you?"

"I ok, thank you, Miss," he replied.

"Don't you like PE and games?" I asked.

"Yes, Miss, I do. But I can't do today. I have bad leg."

"Oh, I see. What has happened?"

"My leg," he said, "it is burnt."

By now, alarm bells were ringing in my head, and I was concerned that our young man had had an accident and hurt himself and I was worried by the fact that he either hadn't been able, or felt able, to tell his teacher or, indeed, any adult. "I am going to take you to get some help," I said.

He looked miserably at the ground and shook his head. "No help," he said. "You can't help."

"I am sure we can do something to make it better," I insisted. "We must check that you don't need to go to hospital."

We continued walking in silence and arrived at my office. What happened next is etched on my memory. The young man rolled up one of his trouser legs to reveal horrific scars from a burn that had destroyed not only skin but muscle too. The leg from the knee down was approximately half the size it should have been.

"Can you tell me what happened?" I asked.

He proceeded to tell me about his home village and how members of the Taliban had taken it over. He had been in his family home when some liquid was thrown through the front door which swiftly ignited. He had been unlucky enough to be close to the flames and his leg was severely burned. But he was luckier than other members of his family who did not survive this attack.

I have shared this story with folk over the years and it has been met with a range of responses. Some have accused me of being naive and a sucker for a sob story, others were saddened and shocked. Of course, I couldn't verify the story and the account above was put together from the boy's limited English. But he was a child who had suffered a terrible injury, was living far away from his family and was doing his best. Frankly, that was enough for me, and I was not inclined to judge or be cynical. To me, once you became a Central boy, you were a Central boy.

Carol Shayle was a fabulous member of the Central staff team, who worked tirelessly with these new arrivals. Over the years, she worked miracles and was totally committed to securing the best futures for those boys. Several went on to further education, including to university, and many are now dads and husbands working locally and, in several cases, running their own businesses. I am always delighted to bump into former students and have a chat about what they are doing now and how life is treating them. I have a particular soft spot for those young men who joined us from some of the most challenging and frightening backgrounds.

Goodbye

I spent many of my happiest years as head of Central Technology College and the community that we built together was incredibly special. When I arrived, the school had lost its pride and reputation and was failing in every possible area. With strategic guidance and support from fantastic colleagues from Ninestiles Federation and our supremely dedicated chair of governors, Central was transformed into a school that could lend a helping hand to others, send its young men out into the world with qualifications and qualities that enabled them to thrive, and which went from a narrow squeak away from special measures to an Ofsted rating of 'good' within fifteen months. To this day I meet former students and I am delighted every time. One of the best examples of this was in 2017 when I returned to work with the academy formed from Central and another local school. On my first day, I met two former students who were now teaching at the academy. That was very special, although it did make me feel old! I have so many fond memories of colleagues and students. Many tears were shed on my last day, as we all said goodbye. The end of Central was like a bereavement and one that took an exceedingly long time to get over. In truth, I have never really got over it. The experience and happiness it gave me were what sustained me in my next headship and, believe me, I needed every ounce of sustenance!

The jewel in the crown of North London

As I dragged my suitcase up the steps leading to the school entrance, I had the distinct impression that this was not the place for me. I stayed for seven long years at the helm at that school and, as we often said in that particular corner of north London, like dog years, seven years was like…well, you get the idea.

How did I end up there and why did I stay so long? In all honesty, it was probably a combination of pride, obstinacy and sheer foolishness. Over the years, I have told many of the colleagues I have mentored to follow their gut instincts and, when they felt a job wasn't right for them, walk away. If only I had followed my own advice!

I stood in the grey, yawning mouth of the north wing entrance to the school. Yes, it was such a large school that it had two wings and, as I discovered, never the twain would meet. That was something I wouldn't fully appreciate until some months later but, for now, I was here to interview for the headship of Fortismere, one of London's most prestigious state schools, described by the outgoing head as "the jewel in the crown of north London". That is a matter of opinion and, at times, it felt more like a poisoned chalice.

As I waited for someone, anyone, to greet me and get the day started, I had a nervous feeling rather like one gets prior to undergoing an unpleasant dental procedure. I noticed the cold, grey tiles on the floor, the scruffy lockers, the lack of displays anywhere and I felt an overwhelming wave of longing for Central, with its familiar smell, bright displays, carpeted floors and warmth. Why was there nobody here to meet me and how was it that I was able to wander into the school unchallenged? Warning bells were going off but, as I was to discover, this was the least of the problems that lay ahead. Eventually, the chair of governors arrived and shook hands with all of the candidates as we assembled nervously. He then set off at quite a pace up the next set of stairs which led to the echoing chamber that was the north wing. I was left behind to drag my suitcase and so began the first day of interviews.

The day of the interview was a blur of mini panels, presentations, awkward coffees and buffets clutched in shaking hands. The adrenaline had kicked in by the time I was put in front of my first panel and I rose to the challenge. I have always been good at interviews but not, it would appear, so good at making that most critical decision about whether the role and setting would be a good fit. We were whittled down to three candidates for day two and asked to set out our vision for the school over one year and over three years. The dilemma at this point of an interview is always how direct to be about what needs to change. Governors, particularly parent governors, can be very sensitive to any implied criticisms, and I have known many colleagues who have had an absolutely hideous time with boards that would not accept or support their vision. This was not the case for me, and I set out my evaluation of the school and what it needed. This must have resonated with panel members, as I was offered the job. Reader, I accepted it...

Always the bridesmaid...

Something I should tell you is that one of the trickiest dynamics you can encounter as the incoming head teacher, is working with the deputy head who wanted your job. This was my fate and one that I was blissfully unaware of until sometime after my appointment when I visited the school and met my senior team for the first time. On reflection, I should have worked out that the absence of key members of the senior team throughout the interview process was highly unusual and should have set alarm bells ringing. I will never forget the first time I met the full team and, I am happy to say, I have never experienced such bristling hostility as that displayed by one of the deputy heads that day.

The PA of the outgoing head had told me to go to the south wing entrance. I had not seen any part of that end of the school during my interview, as it was closed while that curse of so many schools, asbestos, was removed. As I hovered in the reception area, I was aware of a chill in the air and got the distinct impression that I was not welcome. Another call came into the busy reception area and one of the office staff suddenly looked up at me with a strange expression.

"Yes, yes she is here. Can I ask who is calling please? Certainly, I will pass you over."

I was summoned to the hatch and the phone was passed through. It was one of my deputies from Central where I was still the substantive head.

"Is everything ok?" I asked.

"Well, not exactly," he said. "We've just had the call. Ofsted are coming in tomorrow."

Brilliant, I thought to myself. Just what I need. However, all was not lost, and I thanked my lucky stars that I had received advice from my union some weeks earlier that if a school is undergoing an academy conversion, as Central was, it could not be inspected. There was a bit more to it than that but that was the general gist of it. I told my deputy not to worry and I would sort it. I won't bore you with the details but, suffice to say, while navigating my way through the first meeting with my new team, I contacted Ofsted, alerted them to the error and got the inspection cancelled. Stressful? Just a tad!

After the call, I waited a further fifteen minutes or so. A harassed-looking woman came into the reception area and asked if I was Helen.

I confirmed and she said, without a shadow of a smile, "You're supposed to be in the north wing. We've been waiting for you."

I apologised but stood my ground, explaining that I had been asked to report to the south wing. I received no response and so began an awkward trot down to the north wing to meet the team. I was reminded of my first impressions upon arriving for my interview some weeks before.

Perhaps you have encountered this behaviour in colleagues but, for me, it was an unwelcome first. I was ushered into a small office and greeted by my new team, who all sat around a circular table with their arms crossed. I remember them all sitting there like that, but that is perhaps a trick of my memory. However, of one thing I am certain – the deputy head, who I had not met on the day of the interview, sat sideways onto the table, arms tightly folded and looking very deliberately off into the distance. His gaze did not shift a millimetre and he exuded utter fury. I noted this in the fraction of a second it takes to read the room and I also noted that others in the room were clearly not comfortable with this silverback behaviour.

An awkward but useful meeting ensued, and it confirmed my view that the school, led by this senior team, was in need of warming up and the dynamics at play needed to be dealt with, head on if necessary.

New girl

I slept badly the night before my first day and had one of those horrible recurring dreams that are a precursor to stressful situations. I said goodbye to my daughters the evening before and drove up to London from our family home in Gloucestershire. The girls would be looked after in the week by a paid carer while I lived in a flat on site at the school for the first year. My eldest daughter was halfway through her A levels and didn't want to change schools and my youngest was in Year Four. Looking back, I was absolutely mad to think that this way of living and working was sustainable, but I was very driven back then and reacted like a salmon swimming upstream when faced with obstacles. My daughters and I paid a high price for that decision and, if I had my time back again, I would not have put us through it.

As head of Central, I was used to a small staff body of thirty-four. I knew each of them very well and we had been through the fire together, so the bond was strong. My first staff briefing at Fortismere was quite different. Over 130 teaching staff and over eighty support staff were waiting for me in the hall and all eyes were on me. I felt my heart beating fast and had that out-of-body sensation that comes with a panic attack. I had suffered from those on and off over the years and this was a big one. I had the sensation of falling and wondered whether

I would make a spectacular entry to headship by fainting on day one. I didn't, of course, and I suspect that my audience was none the wiser.

The first time you talk to your new staff body is always strange. You are presenting on a topic, i.e. the school, that your audience knows far better than you do, and it is a hard line to walk between setting out your vision for what the school could be and needs to be and keeping the staff on side as you do so. My presentation seemed to be well received and there were smiles and nods in the right places, but this was just the start.

It was a full and tiring day and it flew past in a blur of new faces, meetings, messages from local authority personnel, parents and a range of other people. I realised early on that I was very much on probation and, judging by the lobbying from various groups within the staff and parent bodies, I would quickly find myself in a no-win situation with so many polarised views and demands.

I returned to the flat that was to be my weekday home. It was nicknamed 'the penthouse' and for those who visited it, the irony soon became apparent. It was basic and dreary but convenient. At some point, it had been a classroom and then the caretaker's flat. It had pillars in strange places and single-glazed windows that rattled in the wind and froze on the inside in winter. The main water tank for the north wing was on the roof and I was genuinely fearful that one day it would come crashing in and crush me, drown me or both! I also discovered that discarded bits and pieces, particularly screws and nails from the Design and Technology classrooms destined for the skips didn't always make it and I went through a fair few tyres in the years that I lived in the penthouse! It was not all bad though, and I enjoyed watching the gambolling antics of the family of foxes that lived on the edge of the car park and enjoyed the cheerful chatter of the parakeets that lived in the nearby trees.

Rome and Constantinople

For every yin there is a yang and so it was with my deputies. As hostile as one was, the other could not have been more welcoming. She gave me an enthusiastic rundown of the school's interesting alumnae and parent body, and exuded a real passion for the school. It was only when I asked her about her colleague deputy that her demeanour changed and she explained that he had applied for the headship twice, been denied an interview the second time and was kept strategically away from candidates because he had gone out of his way to be obstructive following the governors' refusal to interview him. Clearly, there was no love lost between the two deputies, but I reminded myself that this was only one take on the story. When she cheerfully described the south and north wings respectively as Rome and Constantinople, I sensed I was in for a very bumpy ride and so it proved to be.

Plus ça change

When I look back to the first weeks and months of that headship, I must smile because I was so confident and determined that I could and would change the default settings of the school. I succeeded in several ways but also had some spectacular failures. The first challenges I needed to tackle were that the school had divided itself into Rome and Constantinople and my two deputies didn't actually speak to each other. I set about dealing with these problems with great enthusiasm. I reasoned that as they were both passionate about the school, were both respected by students and staff alike as really good practitioners and both had a vested interest in the school continuing to do well, they could be bound together. How wrong I was!

I tried reasoning with them, appealing to their sense of common purpose, being blunt about my expectations of them but, apart from a few short-lived truces, the situation didn't improve, sapped energy from the team and made a tough job even tougher. This dynamic had been allowed to fester for several years and I had my suspicions that the flames were fanned by certain individuals who should have known better.

The 'Rome versus Constantinople' situation was critical to shifting this problem, so I took what I considered to be a logical step but which my deputies thought was a step too far. I arranged for whole staff briefings to be held at a midway point on the site. Until now, Deputy One had briefed staff in Constantinople and Deputy Two in Rome. The staff could go for weeks, even months without seeing colleagues from the other wing and consistent messaging was impossible. I still remember those first few whole staff briefings and the folded arms of several staff. There were many, however, who welcomed this change and who saw the importance, and wholeheartedly supported the idea, of a whole staff team. I stuck to my guns and, over the months and years, it became an established norm.

I predict a riot

Rewind, if you will, to the student protests of October 2010. I had been in post for a matter of weeks and knew only a handful of students by name, typically those I needed to speak to! Since taking up the headship, I had attended various events, including an orchestral evening showcasing the considerable talents of the school orchestra. I remembered one of the cellists in particular because of his unusual haircut which, for some reason, struck me as interesting. Little did I know how interesting that would turn out to be.

The student protests against tuition fees were something I and the staff body had every sympathy with. But I could not support or condone students missing school to attend these marches and potentially putting themselves at risk. I made this very clear to students, parents and carers and naively assumed that would be the end of the matter. I had seriously underestimated the political DNA that ran through the school to its very core and was about to find out the full extent of the dissonance.

When the first of many emails landed in my inbox stating "grave disappointment" with me, my decision and my "total lack of understanding that Fortismere is a political school and proud of it", I was non-plussed but thought we'd just have to agree to disagree. Many more emails arrived in a similar vein, but it was when an email arrived that gave me a round ticking off for not "laying on transport" to said protests that I realised I had landed on an entirely different planet! Even writing this, some ten years on, I am as astounded as I was then but, in 2010, I didn't know what I later came to know.

After a rocky day responding to emails through gritted teeth, I returned to my flat and switched on the television. I watched the footage of protests that had tipped over into full-on riots and saw the moment when a young man kicked in the enormous window of a building. Just as I experienced a tightening of recognition in my stomach at a certain memorable hairstyle, my phone bleeped. It was a text arrived from one of my senior colleagues. "Are you watching the news?" I confirmed that I was and texted back, "Tell me I am imagining it, but isn't that 'X' they've just shown kicking in a window?" My colleague confirmed what I suspected, and we talked about what would need to be done and agreed on our approach.

The next day I found myself once again experiencing a mixture of incredulity and utter frustration as I explained to the parent of the student (for it indeed had been one of our students who the whole viewing nation had seen sticking the boot in, literally) that no, I would not lie to the police and that if he didn't ensure that his son handed himself in, he would leave me with no choice but to do so. He tried pretty much every angle from trying to make me take responsibility for "ruining his son's life if he ends up with a conviction" to pleading with me to see it as teenage high jinks. I listened as patiently as I could but would not be persuaded to do something which was illegal and wrong. The upshot was that the young man confessed to the police and received a custodial sentence. You have probably guessed the responses that I received when the local grapevine started pulsing. Once again, I was castigated. This time, I just felt plain angry and recalling that whole sorry episode still makes me shake my head in disbelief.

You really got me

As a teenager, I developed a passion for the mod scene and my hometown of Stroud enjoyed a mod revival in the late 1970s and into the early 1980s. In fact, the scooter and mod scene is still thriving to this day in that part of the world. I spent hours poring over records in Woolworths and in the Trading Post, the town's super trendy record shop. My favourites were Small Faces, The Jam, Secret Affair and best of all, The Kinks. I loved The Kinks and would play and play my albums and I thought the lead singer was simply amazing.

Early in my first term at Fortismere, I inherited a planning challenge linked to the opening ceremony of the new music block, which had been commissioned and built under the previous head teacher but which he had not had the chance to formally open before he moved on. Who could we get to cut the ribbon? Looking into the school's alumnae seemed an obvious starting point and there was quite a range to choose from, including Rod Stewart. But imagine my absolute joy when I read that Ray Davies, lead singer of The Kinks, was an 'old boy'. There was no contest, and an invite was dispatched.

Meeting Ray Davies was a pinch-yourself-to-check-you're-not-dreaming moment. As we leaned over the raised platform at the end of the north wing hall, Ray reminisced about assemblies and the 'bolloc*ings' he'd received from the head teacher at the time. He was interesting, candid and did not disappoint my inner mod! He arrived fashionably late for the opening of the music block and the photo I had taken with him as he cut the ribbon is a treasured possession to this day.

The music block was a fantastic resource and I hoped that many more musicians would be nurtured there. It was a great source of pride and pleasure during my seven years at the school that so many talented youngsters took to the stage in the north wing as Ray Davies had before them. Unfortunately, it was also the case that the music block became a focus for thieves, and we had several break-ins that were both distressing and disruptive. The most dramatic was when the group who targeted the block used what must have been enormous industrial cutters that literally cut a hole in the side of the building to gain access. It looked like someone had taken a giant tin opener to it. While this was infuriating and upsetting, we were all rather fascinated by this ingenious approach and that morning break found many of us, students and staff alike, gathered in front of the gaping hole in the side of the music block.

Blue Monday

With such a large student population, there was always the stark statistical likelihood that the school community would experience a death. At the point of my arrival as head teacher, one of our students was already gravely ill and the prognosis was bleak. He battled bravely and, when he could, spent time in school with his peers. It was raw and sad and took its toll on staff and students alike. Living away from my own daughters as I did in 2010 and 2011, seeing this young man being supported by his family and dropped off at school made me want to hold my own children tightly and missing them caused actual physical pain.

The autumn term rolled on and, as we headed into November, it became ever more apparent that our young man was unlikely to live much beyond Christmas. Anyone who has experienced loss through bereavement will understand the anger and sense of utter disbelief at the brutal unfairness of death, particularly when being faced by a child. His year group was noticeably subdued, and we all worried about their collective ability to cope with their grief.

On 1 January 2011, I received a message from one of my colleagues telling me that the student had died. The poignancy of his life ending just as the New Year began was sharp. So began the planning of how to support his family, siblings, his closest friends in his year group and indeed the school community, as all were affected by this. The students agreed on their preferred ways to remember him, and a bench was placed outside the library in his memory. Foolishly, I had not anticipated that the entire year group would want to attend the funeral. I discussed this with my senior team, sought permission from the boy's family and from the parents/carers of those who wished to attend. Over 180 students wished to attend, so this was a logistical as well as an emotional challenge.

The funeral was held on what is known as Blue Monday and everything seemed to conspire to make us feel as bleak as possible. It was cold, the sky was a sullen grey and we were still in the depths of winter. We made our way to the church, which was located in Tottenham, took our seats in the pews and waited nervously for what was to come. The students were incredible and supported each other with kindness and sensitivity. We collectively held our breaths when the boy's youngest sibling was lifted up by her big sister to speak from the lectern because she was too little to reach it. That was the point at which we all broke, and many tears were shed. While I will remember that as one of the most dreadful times in a career that has encompassed most of what life can throw at you professionally, I also recall it as a time when the school community showed many of its best qualities.

The ripples were felt

Schools are like ships and can be buffeted by political storms and local events. Such was the case with the shooting of Mark Duggan in August 2011. It was a shocking series of events and all of us working across the borough of Haringey knew that the ripples would be felt for many months to come. It is a sad fact that Haringey is probably one of London's best-known boroughs because of Baby P and the Tottenham riots. Working there was a real privilege, and it is no exaggeration to say that I was in awe of many of my head teacher colleagues for the significant differences their leadership made to pupils across the borough. They did this against the odds. I continue to feel incredibly sad that, for all its many achievements and great qualities, Haringey is forever linked to two such ugly and tragic events.

September 2011 was a nervous month for all of us and, as each week went past, we heaved a collective sigh of relief that we had got through the preceding days without incident. All of the secondary schools had their own police officers on site, and we were very grateful for their reassuring presence and detailed knowledge of our immediate communities. Given the rage against the police and the scenes that unfolded on our televisions, it was at times difficult to keep communication channels open, remain calm and focused and not succumb to fear. In fact, as it turned out, the day of the inquest verdict was far more turbulent and we certainly felt the very considerable ripples of that day.

What is the difference between a cosmetic surgeon and an Ofsted inspector? One tucks up features and the other...

Prior to applying for the headship, I researched the school and kept returning to the same question – why hadn't the school achieved an outstanding judgement? After all, it had all the key ingredients and there was no obvious reason why it shouldn't be graded outstanding. You will have heard the rather irritating saying, 'Good is the enemy of outstanding', but, in the case of Fortismere, it was true. It had become very comfortable as it was and saw no reason to change. Wrong! I believed then, as I do now, that if you have the capacity to improve, you have a professional and moral obligation to do so for the benefit of your students. A very wise colleague and mentor once said to me, "Schools were invented to educate children, not provide jobs for teachers." Once, during a particularly frustrating episode, I said that out loud to my staff. It went down as you might imagine, but I didn't regret saying it because it needed to be said and was an important statement to make in calling out a deep-seated and unhelpful counterculture that was holding the school back and, in doing so, denying students the best that could be offered.

In November 2011, fourteen months into my headship, the call came – Ofsted would be in with a team of seven. No stone would be left unturned, and I was curious and impatient to see whether the changes made to date and the improved student outcomes would be enough to secure a judgement of outstanding. Despite the attempts of the more militant staff to scupper the outcome through toxic feedback on the staff survey, Fortismere was graded outstanding and the aforementioned coup was swiftly forgotten as all staff, both those who had added to the burden and those who had put their shoulders to the wheel, basked in the glow of the outcome and it made for a very fine end to the term. The lead inspector contacted me on 19 November 2011 to inform me of the outcome. That was unusual, as it was a Saturday. It was also my 45th birthday and I cannot think of many better birthday gifts!

How did parents and carers react to the fantastic news? I received two emails offering congratulations to the staff and myself and seven which went along the lines of "Just because you have been judged as outstanding doesn't mean that I am satisfied with X, Y, Z." To put that into some sort of numerical context, we had at the time approximately 1,300 families and a student population of more than 1,600. You may be surprised by this response and the paucity of positive messages, but I had already come to recognise this as the default position of the school's parent body. There were so many supportive and positive parents who genuinely rooted for us but, all too often, they were the silent majority and were crowded out by the vociferous and powerful minority who used their professional connections, local influence and clout to push their own agendas. I hadn't encountered this in my first headship and have only seen it in small pockets in schools I have been involved with since. It is ugly and has no place in educational settings but, sadly, it exists. I do not underestimate the importance of being able to contextualise the behaviour of some parents and that has prevented me from succumbing to cynicism. By strange coincidence, I met the lead inspector some years later while heading to Balham on the Northern Line. We recognised each other across the carriage and were soon chatting away about the inspection, the attempt by some staff to sabotage the outcome and what we had been up to since that visit in 2011. It was a really helpful conversation, and I found the candour of the discussions we had very enlightening.

And then they came for me

On 12 December 2011, some Fortismere colleagues and I were privileged to attend a performance of *And then they came for me* staged at the Russian embassy. The play was written by Eva Schloss, an Austrian-English survivor of the Holocaust. In 1945, she and her mother were freed from Auschwitz by Soviet troops. Eva and Anne Frank had played together as children and, after the war, her mother married Anne Frank's father, which Anne tragically did not live to see.

The performance was extraordinary. It interspersed actors presenting scenes from Eva Schloss's life and suffering at the hands of the Nazis with video footage of interviews with other survivors projected onto a screen behind the actors. This made for an enormously powerful experience but what pushed this to another level was the presence of Eva Schloss herself, sitting in the front row of the audience. I watched her from my position a few rows back and wondered how she felt watching her own story being played back to her. What emotions would this stir and how was she able to remain so composed? Afterwards, she enthralled us all during a Q and A session. She talked very candidly about her views on forgiveness and we were all struck by her honest answer that no, she had not forgiven her captors and nor would she.

Anniversary

Back when specialisms were valuable commodities for schools because they brought significant funding with them, Fortismere managed to acquire a number of these, including a modern languages specialism. The languages department was extremely well led and was home to talented staff who were passionate about language teaching. We taught the usual French, Spanish and German, but the introduction of Mandarin prior to my arrival was a very shrewd move. It took time, but the reputation for excellent teaching and an interest in partnering with schools in China led to fantastic opportunities for both staff and students. The Beijing exchange programme was one such extraordinary opportunity.

In May 2012, we boarded a plane for Beijing. This was the first trip to China for all but one of us and we were excited and nervous in equal measure. After an awfully long flight, we arrived in that dreamlike jet lag state, but no sooner had we cleared customs than we were whisked off on our first of many cultural visits and trips. Much of the first couple of days are now a bit of a blur, but I remember all too well one evening very early in the exchange. We had emphasised to the students the importance of eating, drinking plenty of water and trying to go to bed and sleep in line with local time. Most managed this perfectly well but one student was struggling with homesickness and lack of appetite. The host family was concerned that she wasn't eating, and that she appeared pale and withdrawn. As the days went on, she became more and more quiet, and we grew increasingly concerned and decided a visit to see a doctor was necessary. We took her to the extremely basic A & E department of the local hospital. We were greeted by the sight of people in various states of distress on beds in corridors or making do on hard chairs. We were feeling less confident by the minute. Fortunately, our native Chinese speaker took charge, and our student was seen. As suspected, her faintness was caused by lack of food and low blood sugar. We were instructed to direct her to eat and, when we left the hospital, we went to the nearest mini-supermarket and loaded her up with snacks so that even if she struggled to eat the food her host family served her, at least she would get some calories in. I still remember the mixture of fascination and revulsion we experienced when we spotted a display stand, rather like those that display postcards, but containing vacuum-packed chicken's feet for nibbling on. We decided to stick to crisps and savoury crackers. As she settled in and relaxed, so her eating picked up and we were also able to relax.

Fortismere had a well-established link with its partner school in Beijing and the exchange trip became an annual event. Students studying GCSE Mandarin were encouraged to participate and they did, with great enthusiasm. During the course of our ten-day visit, we had some truly remarkable experiences.

Travelling around Beijing is relatively easy and the underground system is very slick with the added advantage of really good Wi-Fi. This turned out to be a blessing! Our group of three staff and twenty students set off for a day of sightseeing and souvenir shopping in the city. We counted everyone on and off the buses and insisted that the students stay close. All went smoothly until almost the last leg of our journey at the end of a busy and tiring day. We were packed onto the underground train bound for our final stop of the day. When the train stopped and the doors opened, one of our students, for reasons best known to him, hopped off and was soon swallowed up by the waiting crowd on the platform. The transport system in Beijing is super efficient and there was no hanging about and no passengers had to be asked to 'stand clear of the doors please', as so often happens on the London underground. Everyone was compliant, the doors closed, and we were off before we could even draw breath. I felt like I was dreaming a horrible dream. What the hell were we to do? Should we stay on at the next stop and hope our student rejoined us or should we go back to the previous station on the basis that he might have waited for us there? We urgently and rapidly discussed this and agreed that our Chinese national teacher would return to the previous stop while the rest of us dismounted and waited for her to rejoin us. What we did have on our side was a Wi-Fi connection, but it turned out to be not terribly helpful as the student we'd 'mislaid' hadn't brought his phone out. Great!

Happily, our plan went smoothly, and we were reunited with our lost sheep. The relief for all was immense and once we got over the fear of 'what might have happened' we were able to tease him and all laugh about this mishap. In all honesty, I still experience a frisson of fear when I think back to that episode. One further twist in that tale was that two years later that young man became head boy!

Those of you who have had the privilege of visiting China will be familiar with certain etiquette that is expected and with very different views about spontaneity and deviating from planned programmes. Of all the cultural differences we experienced, it was the latter that both the students and I found hardest to deal with. We were, however, particularly fortunate to have our Chinese national member of staff with us and she was simply brilliant at negotiating the often tricky terrain between what our hosts expected us to do and what we actually wanted to do. One such example was the famous Water Cube stadium at the Olympic Park.

We had a wonderful visit to the Olympic Park. The students hired Segways, which were a big hit, and they spent a very happy hour riding around an Olympic track. When we came out of that particular venue, they spied the Water Cube which was spectacular on television but, 'in the flesh', it simply took our breaths away. To cut a long story short, it had been converted into a huge indoor water park for public use. Needless to say, the air soon resounded to pleas of, "Please can we go, Miss?" I didn't see why not, but I could see that my colleague was looking a little anxious as she clearly anticipated strained diplomatic relations ahead as this was not in the programme. I suggested that if we also took the Chinese partner students with us that might be a more attractive proposition for all concerned. And that is exactly what we did later in the week. The students had a fabulous time while my colleagues and I sat in a strategically placed café from where we could oversee them. They were having an absolute ball and I sensed we would have trouble extricating them later. Imagine our surprise when we suddenly saw a band walk onto a stage on the far side of the biggest swimming pool with huge speakers perched precariously close to the edge of the stage. The band began to play and they were very loud indeed! We looked at each other and laughed at this bizarre turn of events and how totally unfazed the students were as they shot down terrifying water slides to a backdrop of heavy rock music. The Forbidden City, the Summer Palace and the Great Wall of China could not compete with this, and it was declared "the best thing ever" as we travelled back to base later in the afternoon.

Our partner school was handily close to Tiananmen Square and, as luck would have it, if luck is the right word, we had arranged to visit the Forbidden City and Tiananmen Square on 4 June. Hindsight is, as they say, a wonderful thing. To be fair, we didn't set the programme and we were perfectly content to visit that day. To be fair, nothing could have prepared us for the events that were about to unfold in front of our very eyes.

Fortismere School is situated in Haringey but, what is of more significance in the context of this visit, is that the school has always prided itself on its liberal values. This was something that ran through the DNA of the school, its staff, students, parents and carers. Students did not wear a uniform unless you counted the obligatory Converse trainers they all wore and I think I would have found myself up in front of the European Court of Human Rights if I had ever tried to introduce a uniform. Student voice was 'big' at Fortismere, and parents/carers expected considerable autonomy for their offspring. The 'c' word was also banded around a lot and, in case you are wondering why

I tolerated such offensive language, I should reassure you that the 'c' word I am referring to is consultation! As you will understand, Tiananmen Square with its recent history was both the best and worst place for our students to be on such a key day and date.

The Forbidden City was an eye-widening experience and the sheer scale of it and the knowledge that it was built by human hands was pretty mind-blowing. However, the detailed explanations given to us by the guide were very lengthy and I became aware of our youngsters shuffling about and starting to glaze over a little. It was time to unleash them for a leg stretch and so we headed out into the square.

"Miss, Miss, is it ok if we ask those security guys if we can have a photo taken with them?" I said it was ok, but they had to ask in Mandarin and not be offended or surprised if their request was either ignored or refused. They trotted off happily and within minutes they were posing with big smiles as the security officers stared ahead stoically as the selfies were taken. The scene changed in a matter of moments as we saw a young woman throwing leaflets in the air and shouting in Mandarin. The two security guards were on her, literally, and we watched in horror as she was dragged roughly for a few metres across the paved square to a security van. The back doors of the van were yanked open and she was thrown in. The doors slammed shut and the van sped off across the square. This attracted a lot of attention and our students were clearly shaken and upset by what they had just seen. It was a very sobering reminder of what it is like to live somewhere where neither freedom of speech nor the rights of the individual are the order of the day. I do not remember how long we stood there taking this in. It may have been five minutes or more, but what happened next is something I will never forget. From loudspeakers mounted around the edges of the square, everyone was instructed to leave.

"Do we really have to go?" the students asked, looking bewildered.

"Definitely. Come on."

We set off at a brisk pace, as did everyone else, and I mean everyone. Imagine trying to clear a public space in London with no explanation but every expectation of total compliance? The 109-acre square was emptied within minutes and, when you bear in mind that it hosts 100,000 visitors on an average day, you will appreciate the significance of that.

On the way back to our partner school, the students were subdued and clearly troubled by what they had seen. "What do you think they will do to that young woman?" they asked. "Will she go to prison?" "Will she be tortured?" "What had she even done wrong?" These were just some of the questions to which we had no real answers and what we suspected of her fate we kept to ourselves.

Remember, remember...

When I first took up the headship at Fortismere, if you had asked me what the students would list as the top three accomplishments by which to judge my success, I think it would have been rather different to the reality. I would have said, good progress and outcomes for all, an impressive Ofsted rating and improvements to the site and, in particular, improving the flooded playing fields that thwarted the PE department every autumn and winter. I set about bringing those changes to fruition and succeeded in part with the first challenge and succeeded fully in the case of the latter two. However, while the students and staff were undoubtedly chuffed about the playing fields remaining usable throughout the year, the outcomes were an expected given and the Ofsted rating, while exciting at the time, soon lost its sparkle. What the students really wanted from me, in no particular order, was an annual fireworks display, the swimming pool to be brought back to life and everything else to be kept pretty much as it was. I am sad to say that I never managed to get their much longed-for pool back in action despite many, many tortuous meetings to discuss it. Of all the things that I could have left as my legacy, the pool would have been the most celebrated, but it was not to be and the stagnant waters of the pool continued to glint at me through the fence with mocking regularity. Maintaining the status quo was never really in the plan so, over the years, the students had to acclimatise to changes, but they were generally very sensible and got on with what was asked of them. I do not underestimate that quality in the Fortismere students and will always remember them with fondness and respect. Where I did have a small success was with the much asked for fireworks display. After all, what could possibly go wrong?

I was approached early in 2010 about the possibility of a fireworks display. I didn't feel the time was right and, realistically, with stiff competition from Ally Pally's annual display, the timing would require careful thought. It came up again the following year and, again, we didn't go for it, but the seed had been sown and, to get a range of views on this, I talked it through with my team. They were, as always, earnest in their discussions and posed useful questions and worst-case scenarios, of which there were many to consider! For all that, we decided to go ahead and, in 2012, held our first fireworks display. It was a fantastic event and we were lucky to have some dedicated and well-connected parents and carers to organise it. We had fabulous music, lots of food stalls, a steam fair and, of course, amazing fireworks! The crowd 'oohed and ahhed' in unison and it was an almost fairy-tale event. However, just like all traditional fairy tales, there was one disgruntled 'fairy' at the party. Consider, if you will, the very clear advice we issued about wearing 'sensible footwear' to the event. This was emblazoned on our website and on posters advertising the event. Now you and I have clear ideas about what that might mean given that the ground was likely to be slippery with mud from hundreds of feet and the fact that it was November. Wellie boots, sturdy walking boots, old trainers were the order of the day. But Crocs…with no socks…in November mud… really??? Perhaps it was inevitable, as we never seemed far away from litigious individuals at Fortismere, and sure enough, within days of what had been a fabulous and fun event, the letter warning of legal action arrived. I won't bore you with the details or the rather pathetic attempt to extricate money from our public liability insurance, but I will say that it was a most unpleasant missive, full of threats to sue us. Given that it was a fundraising event for a local school and we had thrown open our doors to the community, it seemed incredibly mean-spirited of this individual to try to make a fast buck from us. Happily, the attempt at litigation wasn't successful and the choice of footwear proved the undoing of that particular bad fairy!

Born to teach

I have sat through a lot of careers talks, conferences and 'events' but I don't think I have ever heard teachers or leaders in education talk about teaching as a career at any of these forums. You must wonder, why is that? For years we have heard about the shortage of secondary maths teachers and other subject professionals have teetered on the edge of extinction during the three decades I spent working in education. It seemed logical to me that, to encourage youngsters into the profession, it would make sense to talk to them about the opportunities teaching offered and to give it the same focus as other professions. We started to do this in a fairly creative way at Fortismere.

Charles Loades, headmaster of Creighton School in the 1970s, wrote a book about his experiences over the sixty years he spent in education. The book was called *Born Teacher* and it was this that inspired the name for the programme I co-devised for students at Fortismere. Creighton School was one of the predecessor schools that became Fortismere, so there was a logic and sentiment behind the programme name too. Interestingly, Fortismere had another book written about it, called *The Creighton Report*, but more of that later.

The enrichment programme I introduced early in my headship was heavily influenced by one we had put in place at Central, but with the number of students to cater for and the number of staff available, we were able to offer a much more impressive programme at Fortismere, with staff stepping up to the challenge. 'Born to teach' was offered to Year Twelve students who were considering the idea of teaching as a career. We approached the Institute of Education (IOE) to ask if our students could attend some of their lectures and if they would certificate the course. They agreed to both requests, and we were over the moon. The course was structured in a similar way to a traditional PGCE with theory sessions and practical experience delivering mini lessons in local schools. I was indebted to local colleague heads who agreed to host our students on their placements. I still remember the afternoon when we took the first cohort to the IOE for their inaugural lecture, delivered by Professor Chris Husbands. On the way back to school on the Tube, our students talked excitedly about the experience which had given them a taste of what it might be like to be at university and had given them invaluable insight into the world of education as a career.

This is a very potted version of what we did and it seems that any school could offer something similar provided it has good relationships with its neighbouring schools to provide placements to practise lesson planning and delivery skills. The lectures or certification are not critical, but they are nice extras and, while there are many different routes into teaching now, we still struggle to recruit and retain new entrants into the profession. At the time of writing, eleven months into a global pandemic, I wonder what further damage has been done to a profession that has been hit particularly hard by the increased demands of new and experimental forms of teaching and learning.

Guardian Soulmates

Some of you may be familiar with the now obsolete online dating site, Guardian Soulmates (GSM). I was single in 2013, having divorced in 2007, and I was keen to meet a partner, as life as a full-time head teacher and single mum, while never boring or unrewarding, could be very lonely. I found myself constantly juggling work commitments while keeping an eye on my eldest who was at university in London and my youngest who was still at primary school. Weekends were a blur of washing, a supermarket shop, responding to emails, and planning for meetings, assemblies and events. The balance didn't feel great as it was mostly work and duty and I had extraordinarily little time to kick back and relax. But I knew that introducing a new man into my daughters' lives would bring its own challenges.

I went on a few dates which were all crushingly disappointing and I came to the reluctant conclusion that this dating business was a waste of time and energy. However, before cancelling my subscription, I decided to give it one last try. I was careful not to give away too much by way of personal details in my profile, so didn't say what I did for a living other than 'education' and located myself in 'London'. I was seriously concerned about the hideous possibility of ending up on a date with the father of one of my students and wondered whether the risk of that happening was worth taking.

I fell into a good-natured back and forth with a chap on GSM and we danced around various topics, such as where we lived. After several messages we arranged to speak on the phone and he told me that he had lived in north London many years ago when he was married. He asked me what part of London I lived in, but I was still evasive and just said "north". He told me that he and his wife and children had lived in Muswell Hill but had decided to get out of London when the time came for the eldest to move to secondary school. I asked him why and he said the reputation of their local school was so poor that they hadn't wanted to send their girls there. He ventured that I might know of it – Fortismere. I sort of saw that coming once he dropped in the Muswell Hill detail. I laughed and said yes, you could say that I knew of the school and that, in fact, I was the head teacher of that fine establishment. He was embarrassed but we both saw the funny side and, of course, his story related back to many years before I arrived in that part of London. Clearly no lasting harm was done as we got married three years later and, by a funny turn of events, as I took his name when we married, the name on the board outside the school that he and his ex-wife had spurned all those years ago was his. That made us both chuckle and did so every time we passed it when walking into Muswell Hill.

If it ain't broke...

One of the most interesting aspects of headship, well, any kind of leadership actually, is making the call for when change is needed. I knew that I would always face some opposition to proposed changes and making changes is often harder in organisations that consider themselves secure. The saying 'if it ain't broke...' has been the undoing of many a school and business, and I followed the Sigmoid curve principle which was vastly different.

Fortismere had run a year group system for years, organised around a traditional horizontal structure. Year groups were quite insular, generally did not mix with each other and assemblies brought out the worst in them, particularly Years Ten and Eleven. Certain traditions and rites of passage had developed over the years which were part of the culture of the school. Some were incredibly unhealthy. For years, the day that Year Eleven embarked on study leave was marked by the students dressing up in fancy dress, setting off fire alarms, disrupting lessons by running through the buildings, knocking on doors and, for the grand finale, heading off into Highgate Woods to get absolutely smashed. In my first summer term, I was told about this by various members of staff, and I couldn't fathom why it was accepted as 'this is what we do around here'. Why on earth would a school want that to be the final memory of a year group and why would students want to spend their final day in barely concealed anarchy? I decided that this was not going to happen and when we got wind, via Facebook, of even more extreme high jinks planned for this year, I talked to my team about how this could be headed off at the pass. We agreed on a plan, but I felt the team was divided into two distinct camps. I was puzzled by the liberal attitude to what I saw as bad behaviour and selfishness and what seemed to be a nervousness about how students, parents/carers and staff would react to any attempt to change this tradition. Those who shared my view seemed relieved that this was finally going to be tackled and lent their influence and knowledge of the school community to the cause.

What happened? Well, it was a fairly hideous day which culminated in the police having to be called, eggs being thrown at staff and about 150 students staging a protest and refusing to leave the north wing. One of my deputies and I went down to speak to the assembled throng. It was intimidating to be faced with such militancy. The students stamped their feet, clapped their hands and called out the names of staff they wanted to be brought to this kangaroo court. It was ugly. It was also public and it was swiftly all over YouTube! Was this the first time such a thing had happened at Fortismere? Not at all and my predecessor had suffered a similar fate when he decided to stop pupils going off site at lunchtime to curb antisocial behaviour in the local area. That year group had staged a sit-in protest, so it is fair to say that Fortismere had 'form' in this department. Perhaps the difference was that while this was a truly horrible experience all around, it did galvanise staff and there was more agreement that something had to change, and change it did.

Vertical

When I first arrived at Fortismere, my plan was to observe, research and then formulate a plan for change. I had gone through a radical structural change at Central when we moved from a horizontal to a vertical system and the benefits had been significant, with older students being offered and taking up opportunities to lead and support younger students, and with opportunities for staff to develop their understanding and expertise as tutors across a range of age groups. That boys' school became a gentler, warmer and calmer place.

For those of you unfamiliar with the terms horizontal and vertical, let me explain. Broadly speaking, schools are usually organised around either year groups (horizontal) with students in age-related tutor groups with a head of year or equivalent who oversees each cohort and related academic and pastoral matters, or year groups are mixed (vertical) so that tutor groups have the full age range of the school which might be Years Seven to Eleven or Years Seven to Thirteen. Heads of house/college, or an equivalent, manage the students and have oversight of pastoral and academic matters. Both systems have their advantages and drawbacks. If you ask me which I prefer, I would say, firstly, that it is determined by the phase that a school is in and its readiness for either system; and secondly, I would throw the question back at you and ask, what are you trying to achieve from an ethos and organisational point of view? If you want a relatively straightforward system that develops expertise in year group-related issues and requirements, go for horizontal, but if you want a school community that mimics family and societal structures and emphasises relationships, then go for vertical.

Fortismere was very firmly in the horizontal camp and, while it is tempting with such a large school to maintain the status quo, I was troubled by several things. Students were poorly behaved in year assemblies, staff sometimes became very stuck in their ways and wanted to only be tutors in the sixth form or for a particular year. While developing expertise in a particular year group has its advantages, it becomes dangerous if assumptions are made that all one needs to do is repeat what one did the previous year or, indeed, the previous ten years! No two cohorts are the same and what works with a year group one year is absolutely not guaranteed to work in the next. The other truth of the matter was that the intake was changing, and the school needed to recognise that and plan to address that change.

I bided my time. How do you create warmth, a feeling of belonging and opportunities to have a voice in such a big school? I was troubled by aspects of the school ethos. It appeared to me that a liberal, middle-class identity prevailed and, while that suited many students well since it was what they experienced at home, it was alien to others and the gap in cultural capital and wider opportunities between the haves and have-nots was significant and growing. The year group structure struck me as problematic as I observed very little positive interaction between year groups and, when they did cross over, it was often older lads dominating football areas or older girls putting younger ones in their place about a range of things that appeared trivial to the adults who had to intervene but devastating to those involved. I was also genuinely concerned by the tensions that bubbled over between students from my school and those who attended a school for the deaf based on the same site. Our students could be thoughtless and unkind, and I saw that enough times to know it was a problem that needed tackling.

As with behaviour, I didn't wade in with a wholesale change to the pastoral structure but quietly made plans in my head and had conversations with individuals over the course of the year. I sent some staff, who were potential ambassadors, to visit schools where vertical tutoring was already established and asked them to report back to colleagues. I also secured the services of someone who was considered a bit of a guru in vertical tutoring, and he came and gave a particularly good pitch to the senior team. The deputy who had been so hostile upon my arrival was still proving tricky and was taking a certain perverse pleasure, or so I suspected, in blocking the changes I was trying to make, so I decided to use 'the poacher turned gamekeeper' model and put him in charge of leading the move from horizontal to vertical. He did a very good job and I look back at that time as the best era of our time working together.

One of my best memories of the planning of this stage was when we met as a whole staff to create the new tutor groups. We assembled in the north wing hall, I issued packs of Post-its and pens and asked staff to use their considerable knowledge of our students to identify individuals who would be a really poor combination in the same tutor group and those who would work well together and bring out the best in each other. Each group would consist of three students from each of Years Seven to Eleven and these would be topped up with a further three drawn from those year groups, making a total of eighteen students per tutor group. We had made the decision the sixth form would join vertical tutor groups for particular sessions, but they would essentially retain their year group identity. In some schools, tutor groups are fully vertical up to Year Thirteen, but we didn't feel that was right for our setting.

The hall was abuzz and the staff threw themselves into this process with gusto. There were peals of laughter and good-natured teasing about some of the suggested combinations but also sensible discussions and pragmatic decisions. Doing the right thing for every student was at the forefront of our planning and taking a good long look at the dynamics at play was both revealing and liberating. Too many schools stick with what they have always done for fear of change or upsetting the status quo but, in doing so, they miss potential that remains untapped and that is a very great shame. The tutor groups that emerged had fascinating combinations and I couldn't wait to see the next stage unfurl.

With such a large structural change, leadership opportunities arose, and this generated excitement, particularly among that layer of staff who were itching to get their teeth into a new challenge. We created six new head of college posts with leadership responsibility for approximately 200 students across Years Seven to Eleven. Years Twelve and Thirteen would be, for the most part, led by heads of year. With the heads of college in place, planning began to bring the students together for the first time. This required a lot of careful and sensitive planning, as the older students, particularly Year Ten who would be the first Year Eleven students in this new system at the start of the new school year, were not exactly thrilled about the change. It is one thing to persuade Year Ten to embrace a change to how their pastoral life looks and feels, but to attempt that with Year Eleven would have been ruinous. As a general rule, when making wholesale changes, I tried to avoid involving Year Eleven and, to an extent, Year Thirteen students. This was good advice that I had been given, and I adhered to it.

To make Year Ten feel special and feel there were advantages for them in this new system, we developed leadership opportunities for them. Their first responsibility was meeting and greeting the new Year Seven students on their first transition days. The Year Tens were dispatched to the north wing where their little compatriots were waiting to be collected. I shall never forget seeing a particularly naughty Year Ten boy leaning down to listen attentively to his Year Seven students who were chirping excitedly at him on their way back to the south wing. I caught his eye; he grinned and then turned his full attention back to his charges. That was pure gold and there were many, many moments like that over the years.

Some of the most powerful aspects of the new system were the smaller tutor groups, with just eighteen students and two tutors per group. The tutors were a combination of teachers and support staff. Not all the staff embraced this change with enthusiasm but the support staff who really got into the new role made an enormous difference and became some of our best tutors. I will never forget the magic moment when the deputy site manager took his tutor group down to the boiler room in the north wing because they wanted to see how big the boiler was and how it worked. He gave them a mini tour, went through the basics of how it all worked and impressed them with his mechanical knowledge. I heard their comments as they came back up the steps: "Cor, that was nuts. It's huge." "I had no idea it would look like that." "I didn't know Sir had to do that to get the heating working." Students' understanding of the contribution that staff made to the school community and environment was undoubtedly enhanced by this change to the way we tutored, and I was enormously proud of the way staff rose to the challenge.

Another opportunity that arose from making this change was finding ways to be more inclusive. I decided that students from Blanche Nevile, the previously mentioned school for the deaf, could and should join the vertical system if they wished and, by agreement with the head teacher and her staff, those who could manage in a mainstream setting with some support joined one of the tutor groups and took part in tutor time, assemblies and the activities and events that those gave rise to. This definitely made a difference and I loved seeing that. I was invited to attend the annual prize-giving event at Blanche Nevile school. I enjoyed this very much, and the head and I became good friends and shared a cup of coffee and a good old putting-the-world-to-rights session several times a term.

So, what happened when Year Eleven left at the end of the first year of the new vertical system? They still dressed up in fancy dress, but the colleges organised leaving assemblies that emphasised the mini communities within each one and their particular memories and highlights. The assemblies were controlled tightly enough to be orderly but relaxed enough to be fun. We had a tea with staff where students could say goodbye properly, get yearbooks signed and undergo a positive rite of passage. To send students on their way, we formed an archway of staff rather like a wedding line-up and clapped the students off site. After going through this ritual for the first time, many staff told me how lovely it had been and how much nicer it was to see youngsters off on a positive note. Over the years, we saw some fantastic costumes and students really took this to another level. In 2013, the year of the

Findus horse meat scandal, one student dressed as a lasagna with horse's head and limbs poking out and others dressed as giant lanyards, in a good-humoured poke at me for introducing lanyards to our otherwise non-uniform school.

Revolution ain't easy

I spent the Easter holidays of 2013 in Havana. I had visited once before with my daughters, but this trip was with a former teaching colleague and our plan was to explore the city and not stick solely to the expected path. A long-held fascination with Cuba in general and Havana in particular was further fuelled by this trip. The memories of that most photogenic of cities, where plants have reclaimed the territory, with trees bursting out through ceilings and delicate ferns unfurling between the crumbling pillars of formerly grand dwellings, remain with me to this day. I was struck by the contrast between two such different interpretations and manifestations of communism as experienced in Beijing and Havana.

When I was at secondary school, I had a particularly excellent history teacher. She was properly academic, well travelled and passionate about her subject. She used to show us slides from her travels to Egypt among other places. We used to be very ungrateful and would titter at her holiday attire but, secretly, I was impressed by her adventurous spirit and recognised, even as a rather thoughtless teenager, that for a woman to travel off the beaten track was something to be admired. It was evident from the photos she showed us that she was driven by curiosity and not held back by anyone who tried to suggest that perhaps these places were too risky for a woman to travel to alone. I think she would have approved of my choice of Havana as a destination.

As my friend and I waited in the departures area of Jose Marti Airport, we decided to have a final bottle of Cristal. We were both very much in holiday mode, dressed casually and with our guards down.

"Hello," a woman said. "I spotted you earlier and just had to come over. My daughter goes to your school. She's over there and would love to come and say hello."

She said this so fast that she hardly drew breath and, before I knew it, I was walking as if sleepwalking towards a teenage girl who looked as if she wanted the airport floor to open up and swallow her. Parents are so embarrassing, and I realised that no matter how far away I was, I was never more than ten feet away from a pupil, or so it seemed! The world shrunk a little that day.

The year of the snake

In May 2013, I was once again Beijing-bound with a group of students and two colleagues. Lest you are wondering whether I ever spent any time in situ, let me assure you that I most certainly did and, believe me when I say that there was nothing glamorous or luxurious about this trip. It turned out to be rather tense and diplomatic relations were strained, to put it mildly!

We landed as before and were immediately whisked off for a day of activities. We had asked that some consideration be given to the eleven-hour flight and significant jet lag, but no, there was a programme that had to be adhered to. I do not mean to sound ungrateful, but if you have travelled with one weary teenager on any kind of a lengthy trip, you can imagine that multiplied by twenty-four! Many of our days out were remarkably similar to the previous year but with a couple of notable exceptions. The trip to visit two schools on the outskirts of Beijing is something I will never forget!

We travelled by coach to the first school and had little idea what to expect, so we had no particular preconceptions. Nothing could have prepared us for what happened. As we pulled up outside the school, we became aware that the entire school was assembled in silence in a sports stadium, the size and magnificence of which any professional football club would have been proud. The pupils stood to attention and we were ushered into the stadium under the watchful eyes of 1,000 pupils and the full staff body which must have numbered 150. All eyes were on us, and I realised with horror as I was ushered towards an ornately decorated top table, that a speech was expected. I was not prepared for this. My students looked at me with a mixture of pity, amusement and expectation.

"What are you going to say, Miss? Did you know you were going to have to speak?"

I smiled with affected confidence and breezily said, "I'll be fine. I always have a few words ready."

That was total bullshi* of course, but there was no place to hide so I had no choice but to speak. The next few minutes are a blur, but I got through it. We were then treated to what can only be described as a dazzling display of martial arts, opera singing and calligraphy. Each section was executed to perfection and the youngsters must have been practising for weeks. What transpired next was both hilarious and horrifying. As the final performer took his seat back in the stadium, expectant eyes turned to us, and I realised with absolute, stomach-churning certainty that a performance was now expected of us. Now it was my turn to look amused yet pitying. All I can say is that my students brilliantly rose to the challenge with a medley of songs they had prepared on the coach following a hint that this might be expected. Were they as slick as our hosts? No. Were they able to execute each song with precision to rival the opening ceremony of the Beijing Olympics? They were not. But, my goodness, I was so proud of them, and they received a deafening round of applause and were rightly delighted. We certainly laughed a lot about this experience on the way back to base and it was a bonding experience for all of us. However, this was not the only memorable experience that day. The other will remain with me forever as a most bizarre incident indeed.

It transpired that the other school we travelled to that day prided itself on its horticulture. There was nothing wrong with that and, indeed, Fortismere also boasted a plot of land where tasty things were grown. However, what was quite different was the seriousness with which the 'introductions' to the cucumber plot were made. We were lined up off the coach and ceremoniously filed to the plot where the cucumbers were grown. Our native Chinese speaker was put to effective use and translated the specific instructions that we were duty-bound to follow. We each had to pick the cucumber of our choice, move to the washing station, immerse our cucumber in water and eat it. This, in itself, may not sound particularly strange, but the sight of twenty-four teens, solemnly clasping their cucumbers, washing them carefully and then delicately nibbling on them was very funny. As the saying goes, if you can't beat 'em, join 'em and each of us in the teachers' group also plucked a cucumber, washed it reverently and nibbled through its surprisingly spiny skin.

Pop-up

2013 was very much the year of flash mobs and pop-ups. I remain sadly disappointed to this day that despite living in London for eight years between 2010 and 2018, I never witnessed a flash mob in action. While travelling up and down the Northern Line I used to wonder, is today going to be the day? It never was. However, when it came to what could be done at Fortismere, there was no reason why flash mobs and pop-ups could not be a feature of the year ahead and, so, I began to work with interested staff on how we could incorporate these elements. We had various successes over the year, but my personal favourites were the guerilla knitting that appeared on trees in the south wing, a fabulous trompe l'oeil drawn in chalk by one of our tutors and his tutees which showed what appeared to be a huge hole that had opened up in the ground with a group of youngsters peering into it, and small paper figures displayed on walls and tucked away under window ledges. Traces of these could still be seen two years after the project ended.

The other, less welcome 'pop-up' which happened was a no-notice Ofsted inspection on the first day of the autumn term. To be honest, I had thought the urban myths about 'we are in the car park ready to inspect you' were just that, myths. Apparently not…

I was out on morning duty in the south wing, pottering about, chatting to students, and encouraging them to make their way to period one before the bell went. All was well and it was a good first day back after what had been a lovely summer. I hopped and skipped my way upstairs to my office where I was met by my somewhat ashen PA. "Helen, we've been trying to get hold of you. Ofsted called. They are on their way." No kidding! They were indeed on their way and were, in fact, just ten minutes away waiting for a taxi to bring them to the site. Why were we being inspected, having been graded as outstanding in 2011 with an upward results trend? I cannot really say too much, as it would undoubtedly breach some General Data Protection Regulation (GDPR) or related policy but, suffice to say, it was triggered by a parental complaint. That wasn't unusual at Fortismere, as we regularly received 'feedback' from parents on how we might do things better, but this was on a whole other level. When Ofsted comes a-calling, you experience, or at least I always did, an almost dreamlike state where time seems to slow down, and every word and action takes on a weight and significance that it wouldn't otherwise. As head, I was acutely aware of the weight of expectation on me and how the impact of a poor and negative outcome would affect so many. I also knew that establishing an honest and open dialogue with the lead inspector was critical. I learned from my former executive head that you must fight your corner, be thoroughly prepared and, when a metaphorical stone is turned over, be ready. Better still, don't let yourself be in a position where you are caught off guard. Apart from that, it's a walk in the park...

The inspectors came, carried out their inspection and left at the end of the day completely satisfied that there were no grounds for concern. It was incredibly stressful and, added to that, we felt pretty aggrieved that a parent could put a whole school through an inspection on spurious grounds, but Ofsted has a job to do and they did it. The lead inspector was fair, helpful with her advice and an expert in her field. When I met her again recently, I felt comfortable and it was nice to catch up on what had transpired since we last met.

And what of the day to day?

Of course, headship is not all about extremes and trips away and much of my time was spent establishing expectations, structures and systems to propel the school forward and really see what could be achieved. A lot of my time was also spent walking the site, taking the daily 'temperature', and being seen. In terms of the latter, I could never win. If I was in the south wing, I was accused of not being visible in the north wing, and vice versa. One of the ways I tried to deal with this was to base myself in the north and south wings on alternate weeks. That helped a bit and I enjoyed switching locations and being more accessible so staff could just drop in for a chat or a grumble or to share an idea. Many did drop in and that was particularly important to me. As head, I had to frequently remind myself that the way people saw me bore little relation to how I saw myself and how I felt. I have been told that I always looked at ease when addressing audiences, but the truth was that I would suffer from dreadful palpitations, light-headedness and a rather unpleasant out-of-body sensation in the build-up to the first few minutes of speaking in public. I am also naturally quite shy and, so, perhaps not really suited to a role that required so much of the public self. While it is commonly said that we look to be respected rather than are overly concerned with being liked, I think a more honest and human truth is that we all have a strong need to be liked. I know that I often was not liked at Fortismere and that I made changes and decisions that were not universally popular. If I had my time again, would I have done things differently? In all honesty, no. What I learned in my previous headship was that you can choose to do many of the wrong things but if you select the few right things, changes can be transformational. It is not an exact science and it is not particularly easy to teach others, as much of it is based on instinct and with that, of course, comes risk. So it was with my time at Fortismere.

What changes did I decide to make? I have already alluded to the relationship between my deputies and, although some of the steps I took made the function of their roles better, the dynamic between them never really shifted. In the end, natural processes took over and one retired and the other secured a headship at another school following a strategic restructure. I decided to go for a flat structure and get rid of the role of deputy altogether. The process was fraught and staff were clearly divided about my decision, but this was a battle for the longer term good of the senior team and the school. I was heartened to see the team grow in confidence and we had a lot of fun and good-humoured banter at our meetings while taking very seriously the responsibility for leading the school. The relationship that can develop within a team can be the difference between a job being enjoyable or unbearable and, certainly, the early months were much tougher because of the oppressive vibe exuded by one of the deputies and I was saddened to see how timid many of the team were when it came to speaking their minds. Once they felt confident to do so, it was like working with a brand new team and I became very fond of them to the extent that I remain in contact with several of them to this day.

Many heads want to make their mark on the issue of behaviour, and it is a fascinating aspect of the job. My early impressions were that behaviour was fairly good but could be a lot better and there was an arrogance about the way the students spoke to staff that I really didn't like and did not see any place for. For example, a member of staff might ask a student to move along to their next lesson more quickly. A stock response would be, "I am going as fast as I can and if you hadn't stopped to speak to me, I'd get there much quicker." As I pointed out to staff, they had, to all intents and purposes, been politely told by the student to "fu*k off". Many of our students were far too smart to actually fall into the self-made trap of swearing at teachers but they certainly knew how to press the buttons.

The dress code was another area of conflict. We didn't have a uniform and most students wore perfectly reasonable gear to school. I remember, however, one particular exchange with a young lady in the sixth form. She aspired to be a model and had the height and slender frame to suit that profession. A particular fashion trend that wound us all up was tights with holes and, to be perfectly frank, in some cases there were more holes than tights material! So it was with this young lady and one morning while on gate duty, I took her to one side for a quiet word. She kicked off and protested about my insistence that she go home and change. I stuck to my guns and would not be dissuaded, shouted at into changing my mind or emotionally blackmailed with crocodile tears. In the end, she looked me up and down and with a withering look said, "You're just jealous because you know you couldn't pull off anything like this and look as good." She had me and I honestly did not know whether to laugh or shout. I took the middle ground and firmly repeated my instruction to her to go home and change. She did so very grumpily and while I would love to tell you that I won the battle, I did not and a few days later, she appeared again in what looked like something that had lost several rounds with a very angry cat. We locked horns many more times and each time, I stuck to my guns and she to hers. However, the day finally came when she said to me, "Ok, Miss, you win. I can't be ar*ed to argue anymore."

An assessment of behaviour over the first year of my headship gave me a sound understanding of the issues and pinch points. I think some folk expected me to wade straight in and change things but that was not an immediate priority. I have worked to support schools in more recent times where sorting out behaviour has been the priority because it would be dangerous not to do so. That was not the case at Fortismere. We undertook a thorough survey of staff and student views and were delighted, but not surprised, that behaviours that were barriers to teaching were the same ones identified by students as barriers to learning. Our Behaviour For Learning (BFL) system was built upon those areas of common ground and we set about training staff and students in its language and ways. This took six weeks and ran over the summer term. I chose this time of year to avoid introducing significant changes for Year Eleven students who, as I mentioned earlier, can often be resistant to change, draining staff time and energy. I wanted to ensure that staff and students had a shared understanding of the new system, had contributed to it, and had proper training and opportunities to practise before going live. Was it successful? When Ofsted inspected us in November 2011, behaviour in class was judged 'outstanding' and that was a first for the school.

Solutions not problems

My first impression of the school when I arrived that morning for my interview turned out to be very accurate. The school was made brittle by factions, and these weren't just along the north wing–south wing divide. There was a very deep-seated and unhealthy union culture within the school. I was shocked by the wilfulness of the local union rep and how many staff would put her wishes and instructions above what was right for the students and the school. When I arrived, I was welcomed by the other head teachers from the schools in Haringey. I was warned, "You will get picked off by X because you are new. She does it to all the heads." Did this rite of passage lie ahead for me? I did not much like the sound of it but I put the worry to the back of my mind.

In truth, the early years were fairly hassle-free until I crossed swords with this local union rep over a disciplinary hearing which didn't go the way she thought it should. That marked the change in our relationship from there on. I had seen and heard other heads having to deal with interference, spiteful comments, endless freedom of information requests designed to create enormous amounts of work, nasty personal attacks in the local papers and, a firm favourite of that rep, the Friday afternoon email which was sent to try and ensure a weekend of worrying about whatever piece of mischief she was stirring up. While this may sound like something and nothing, the relentlessness of her focus on certain colleagues was shocking to observe and she did very real damage to relationships between heads and their staff which was the saddest aspect of all this. She rarely if ever focused on students and she seemed to be driven by self-promotion.

I had taken on the role of Association of School and College Leaders (ASCL) rep for Haringey so was inevitably more involved in union matters. I should say that I have always been a union member, I recognise their importance and, indeed, I had taken on a union role. However, I have also always believed that school matters should primarily be dealt with internally wherever possible and a union should be the last resort. This was not the culture I found myself in and, at times, it was totally bewildering.

I had been in Haringey for a few years and had taken on the role of vice chair of the secondary heads' group, which I saw as an important responsibility. I liked my colleagues very much, had reason to be extremely grateful to several of them for the support they gave me when I first arrived and I enjoyed the banter and good-natured ribbing that went on at our meetings. I was in awe of what so many of them had achieved for their students against incredibly challenging circumstances and with many factors against them. Their individual and collective ability to think and plan strategically, while calmly and thoughtfully dealing with the unexpected, was impressive. These individuals were as different from each other as any group of heads could be but what they had in common was tenacity and ambition for their school communities. They were, and are, the real deal and I feel extremely fortunate to have worked with such inspiring people.

We worked collectively to find solutions to problems, but the union rep was a growing problem that we had not yet managed to solve. It was a delicate matter and fraught with political landmines that threatened to detonate. If we pushed too hard to curb her most extreme behaviours, we were accused of trying to bully or undermine unions and workers' rights. If we tried to ignore her, she kept pushing, so, we were caught between a rock and a hard place. After yet another incident we had had enough and we collectively decided to write to Haringey local authority and ask for the rep to be dealt with under the disciplinary code. We agreed that we would withhold payment for the facilities time service level agreement until this was done. Facility time is time off from an individual's job, granted by an employer, to enable a rep to carry out their trade union role. The rep was suspended and so began a very bloody battle. As chair and vice chair of the group, my colleague and I bore the brunt of her wrath and our schools were taken out on strike action in the autumn term of 2014. This caused a hugely damaging rift among staff, parents, students and governors and left scars for years to come. As we entered the third week of strike action, we felt that the time had come to resolve this matter one way or another. It was complicated and time-consuming. The rep was suspended on full pay for a year. She was allowed to continue with any casework started before her suspension and so, in reality, could continue with her string pulling and interference. We were all exhausted and everyone had their own views about how this matter should be handled. The national papers also got stuck in and one week in November 2014 my colleague head and I had the dubious privilege of our schools featuring in all the broadsheets and tabloids. And I mean all! Generally, the papers were sympathetic to the schools rather than the rep and she got quite a hammering, particularly from the *Daily Mail*. Did it sway her? Not a jot.

Living so close to the school and its community was very tricky indeed and never more so than during that period. One evening, my then partner, now husband, and I decided to go to a local pub for a drink and some Thai food. We were there for less than ten minutes when a man approached us, clearly a bit the worse for wear. He asked if he might sit down and join us. He didn't wait for a reply before plonking himself down. He then proceeded to tell me that his kids attended my school and that he wanted to give me some advice on how to manage the strike action. This was both unwanted and inappropriate, so we politely but firmly explained that I was 'off duty' and that we just wanted to enjoy a quiet evening. He muttered something rather huffily and shuffled off. Phew, that was close. But that was not the end of the matter. My partner nipped off to the loo and no sooner was he out of sight than this same man came back and again plonked himself down. By now he was more drunk and a thorough nuisance. I took a different approach and simply ignored him and stared intently at my phone. He did not get the hint and it was only when my partner returned and politely but firmly asked him to leave that he did so. This was not the only incident involving unwanted intrusions that I faced over the years, and I found it strange that parents gave no thought to tackling me about work matters in the supermarket, in the GP's waiting room or at the local park. I hadn't encountered such behaviour before, and nor have I since.

The strikes rumbled on and finally an agreement was reached, and they were eventually called off. Our schools resumed business as usual, but I never felt the same way and had a sense of mistrust and unease around many of the staff. For their part, I am sure they felt the same. As a head, this was not a good position to be in but, much as I was tempted to get as far away as possible, I was not going to be driven out of the school. I would leave when I was ready and when it was the right time for me.

Breathe

The weeks building up to the strike action and its aftermath took their toll. The adrenaline that coursed through the school's veins probably kept us all going in a perverse way but, once the quieter times came, so did the exhaustion. I had known for some time that I was mentally, emotionally and physically tired. I wasn't sleeping, I felt permanently on edge and I found staff briefings a real ordeal as I felt the animosity from certain staff that was not easing while those who were just decent and getting on with the job in hand looked uneasy and were disinclined to challenge their colleagues. I didn't blame them for that. But I was outnumbered, worn out and on my way down.

I had reached the grand age of forty-seven and had never been to Scotland. This was something that needed to be remedied, so my partner and I set off for Edinburgh over the Easter holidays of 2015. We had many adventures, including bumping into Ian McEwan at a boxing match. Either of these facts would, on its own, have been unusual, but the combination of the two was extraordinary.

Within days of returning home, we both succumbed to proper, full-on flu. I am talking teeth-chattering temperatures, aching joints that brought us both close to crying and eyes that throbbed in their sockets. Each night, we awoke in the early hours, unable to sleep, and listened to the World Service. It became such a source of comfort. My partner recovered and was up and about after about a week. I lurched from one chest infection to the next and finally ended up with pleurisy. I remember going into work one day because I had been prescribed steroids and I felt better. That was a mistake. I ended up sitting at the side of the north wing hall, watching an INSET day while trying to get some oxygen into my lungs. It was scary and I was reminded of it recently when listening to the truly shocking stories of Covid patients unable to draw breath at all. What I didn't recognise was that my body was telling me that something had to give. Did I listen? No.

Just as I was starting to get back on my feet in May, we were subject to yet another no-notice inspection. I got out of bed and headed into work to meet the lead inspector. It was a no-win situation. If I had stayed at home, I would have felt absolutely lousy about leaving my team to deal with an inspection, but going in wasn't ideal either as I was far from firing on all cylinders. The inspection went fine and, once again, we retained our outstanding judgement and the team went away satisfied. My Haringey head teacher colleagues often teased me about the frequency of inspections at Fortismere. They would enquire with mock concern, "My goodness, Helen, at least three weeks have passed. Isn't it about time for an inspection?" Ha bloody ha! Actually, I could see the funny side of it and, while I would never say this out loud, as an outstanding school, no-notice inspections were definitely a highly effective way of keeping us all on our mettle. I would definitely categorise them as 'type B fun'.

I arrived home at the end of the two days of inspection exhausted. What on earth was wrong with me? I had been through far worse inspection experiences than this one and the outcome was excellent, so why did I feel so wretched? Certainly, I was still struggling to recover from pleurisy and that wasn't helping, but there was something else wrong and I couldn't quite put my finger on it. I felt uneasy and anxious all of the time.

Protest and survive

2015 was an extraordinary year and, looking back on it now, I must pinch myself. We had a phenomenal run of experiences, any one of which in isolation would have been remarkable and memorable, but to have one after the other was simply astonishing.

The year had not begun in a particularly auspicious way and, to be honest, 2014 had nearly finished me off. Walking the site was still uncomfortable and I dreaded staff briefings, but we kept them going. Perhaps after a storm, some sunshine was due and so it was in the latter part of 2015.

On 17 October, we were all beyond excited as we waited for a special guest speaker to arrive. The hall was set up, technical equipment checked and the audience of sixth formers, the art and photography department team, staff who were lucky enough to have a free period and a few parents and carers waited expectantly. I hovered around in the lobby as part of the welcoming committee. We heard our guest some time before he actually appeared as he made his entrance on a fantastic Harley Davidson. He dismounted, took off his crash helmet and grinned at us. What struck me was that he was polite, punctual and in no way a prima donna. Having experienced Ray Davies' fashionably late entrance some years earlier, I was not overly optimistic that our most recent star visitor would be any better, but he was impeccably well mannered from start to finish.

We led him into the packed hall and could hear the rustling and shushing as we made our way down to the front. The students looked a little surprised, possibly even disappointed, as our guest had come simply as himself and not as his famous alter ego, Claire. Yes, our special guest was Grayson Perry. If the students felt any disappointment that he had not donned a Claire outfit, that soon disappeared, and we all listened, spellbound, for the next hour. One of the most brilliant things about Grayson Perry, and there are many, is that he has the ability to choose just the right lens to look through. Addressing youngsters aged between sixteen and eighteen, he looked at their needs from the perspective of a father as well as a phenomenal artist. This was illustrated particularly clearly when he addressed his choice of attire head-on. He explained that because he wanted the students to really listen to him and not be distracted by looking at what he was wearing, he had deliberately chosen not to come as Claire. The audience nodded and we all agreed afterwards that this was a wise decision. During the Q and A, one student asked him what advice he gives to aspiring artists. I am paraphrasing slightly but in essence, he said, "Turn up on time, be nice to people and finish what you set out to do." He said this without a trace of irony or flippancy, and it was perfectly clear that he meant every word. Again, if students were disappointed by the apparent simplicity and straightforwardness of this, that soon passed, and we all recognised that we had just heard pure gold. Those of us in the hall who were parents found that this advice particularly resonated with us as a guiding principle which, if adhered to, would pretty much get you through life very effectively.

Grayson stayed and talked to students, shook hands, waited patiently while photos were taken and then, with a polite and warm farewell, he was away on his Harley. He was utterly delightful from start to finish and we all basked in the afterglow for days.

I can't say too much at this stage...

Our visit from Grayson Perry had already given us enough excitement to last a term, let alone a month. But some days later, on what started as an unremarkable day, I was trawling through emails when my PA rushed in looking quite flustered.

"Helen, I've just taken a call," she said.

Like I said, so far, so unremarkable.

"A lady from the Foreign and Commonwealth Office just rang. They have asked whether you would be willing to host a VIP visitor but they can't say who it is."

I was puzzled. "What do you mean they can't say who it is? How do I know whether to say yes or not?"

My PA shrugged. Time for a cuppa and a think. The kettle went on and tea was brewed and my PA and I began one of the strangest discussions I have ever had. After some mulling over the possibilities of who it might be, we agreed that if our hunch was correct, this would be nothing short of amazing! My PA was on the case and the visit was agreed. We still did not know who we had agreed to host but, what the hell, we were in now.

What followed over the next three weeks was extraordinary. We consulted with police and security staff used to planning security for royalty and high-profile political figures. We repeatedly walked through the site to make sure there were no weak spots that would make our visitor vulnerable. In addition to thorough checks and regular scrutiny, we were required to put on a programme of entertainment but were not allowed to tell those involved who it was for. It was exciting but incredibly challenging to work on such a top secret but high-profile event and keep the school running smoothly. I remain indebted to my PA and key members of my senior team and the modern languages department who were integral to the planning but did so without questioning why or, indeed, demanding to know who was coming.

There were tensions along the way as expectations about the level of security and the approaches to be taken were, at times, at odds. I shall forever be grateful to a senior member of the Metropolitan Police who provided calm and expert guidance. I nearly choked on my coffee on the day when our mystery visitor's security representatives told me that snipers would be installed on the roof of the north wing entrance. I was totally unprepared for that and it felt very frightening. The wonderful senior Met officer explained to me that, as head teacher, I had the right to refuse this request as it was taking place on my site. I asked what he advised and he said that, in his experience, snipers were not needed and, in fact, they were more likely to increase the risk to all concerned. He recommended that I simply say no. That is exactly what I did.

Sometimes when I recall the events leading up to the day itself, I sense that folk aren't sure whether to believe what I am saying. Sometimes I felt as if I was dreaming the whole thing but, luckily, close colleagues and my partner were there to witness some of these bizarre events, so I know they really happened.

A few days before the scheduled visit, I came out of my flat to find a gentleman of Chinese appearance standing a few metres away from my front door. He was smartly dressed and stood with his arms folded. As I made my way down the road, he followed me at a not particularly discreet distance, and he seemed unconcerned about being noticed. He trailed me all the way to work and then stood by the entrance gate as I went inside. You might say that was just a coincidence and that it meant nothing. But then my partner and I decided to go for a meal at our local

Italian restaurant, something we did often. Not long after we sat down, a party of four Chinese adults turned up and seated themselves at the table closest to ours. They ordered drinks but no food and left when we did. Coincidence? I think not.

The morning of the visit arrived, and the visitor's identity had still not been revealed to staff or students. Only I and key members of my team who were directly involved in working with the Met, Foreign and Commonwealth Office and other parties knew who was coming to visit. Everything was ready and it was time for the final security checks to be undertaken. Two sniffer dogs were led into the north wing and with a command were let off their leads. So began some frenzied sniffing and the dogs were extremely excited but totally focused. They were sniffing for arms and explosives. They continued their busy checks for several minutes and then one stopped in front of one of the students' lockers and would not budge. Its tail was going like the clappers and whatever was in there was driving it into a frenzy. My stomach tightened. Oh God, please don't let there be anything dreadful in there. We were asked to provide the master key to unlock the locker. My heart was in my mouth as the locker was opened. We craned to see what was in there. The dog handler reached inside, rummaged around and then pulled out a rather festering PE kit. A collective sigh of relief and a smile. It seems that 'eau de teenager' is irresistible to a sniffer dog!

With the security clearances completed, we waited with great excitement for our special visitor. We had other guests to welcome, ranging from local authority officers to government officials. Everyone was duly assembled and ready in the welcome line to greet our special guest.

A black car glided into the car park followed by a convoy of others. It's her, she's here! Students were primed and ready and the north wing hall and entrance had never looked so tidy. Please don't let anything go wrong!

The door of the first car opened and out stepped China's First Lady, Madame Peng. She was graceful, impeccably dressed and utterly charming throughout her visit. I said a few words to welcome her and, through an interpreter, Madame Peng responded and spoke to us. The audience was hushed, and I think we all shared a feeling that this could not really be happening, but it most definitely was.

Our students performed songs and poems and showcased a demonstration lesson in Mandarin. Our visitor smiled and looked like she was thoroughly enjoying the experience. The pièce de résistance came towards the end when two students performed one of the songs that Madame Peng herself had been famous for when she was a singer. She looked genuinely moved by that and it was a lovely way to round off the event. She left as she arrived, elegantly moving through the audience, smiling, shaking hands and then she was gone.

Those of us who had worked to bring this event together sat down in the north wing foyer and talked in wonder about what had just happened. Only now could we let the rest of the staff and, indeed, students know who our visitor had been. I am enormously proud of what we achieved that day for two reasons. We managed to run the school day without a hitch so business as usual could continue and we successfully created an intimate learning experience out of what was a very high-profile political event.

The Creighton Report

Fortismere, as you will by now understand, was and is a unique school. Its history, finger on the political pulse and energy are unlike anything I have known. How many schools have not just one, but two, books written about them or, at least, where they feature heavily? Fortismere was not just immortalised in *Born Teacher* which charted part of the school's history but, in 1974, *The Sunday Times* sent the well-known journalist Hunter Davies to spend a year at the school and record events and developments as they rolled out. It is a fascinating and intimate account of a year in the school under its inspirational headmistress, Molly Hattersley.

The ensuing book, *The Creighton Report*, should be required reading for all new entrants to the profession as it offers a valuable lesson in the origins of the comprehensive system. It is also funny, cheeky and endearing in equal part. We were bowled over when its author, Hunter Davies, agreed to come back to the school and give a talk about his 1974 experiences. He came on a November evening in 2015 and we were treated to a most engaging, entertaining and, at times, pretty close-to-the-knuckle talk. We loved it! A couple of years earlier, I had managed to get a telephone number for Molly Hattersley and had a very moving conversation with her. While a little hard of hearing, she was as sharp as a tack, interested to hear about developments at the school since her time and full of wisdom. The conversation is something that I prefer to keep private but, suffice to say, I felt very honoured to be part of the long line of head teachers who had been at the helm of the school in all its various incarnations.

Sigmoid curve

The Sigmoid curve was a philosophy and approach that I learned from Sir Dexter and it was something I tried to apply as much to my personal life as to my professional life. Knowing when change is needed is tricky, to put it mildly. If you think about your own life up until this point, how many substantial changes have you made yourself and how many were forced upon you? As I write this, we are slowly emerging from lockdown with all the significant imposed changes that has brought, in addition to all the ones we may have chosen to make.

Towards the end of 2015 and into the start of 2016, I began considering what I would like to do next with my career. Moving on from a headship is not a decision to be taken lightly and certainly not in the case of a school as large and complex as Fortismere. I wanted to complete the journey with those students who had joined Year Seven in September 2010 and see them through to Year Thirteen. I am sure many of them wouldn't have minded much either way whether I stayed or left as I was probably little more than a distant figure, as much as I tried not to be. However, this was a commitment I had made to myself and I was determined to see this through and begin succession planning. This stage of my career was in many ways the hardest, as planning to leave a role brings none of the excitement of planning the changes you will ring in a new post. While I would never say that my work was done at Fortismere, I felt satisfied that I was leaving it in a strong position with an extremely capable and knowledgeable senior team to lead it.

There are a number of approaches you can take to leaving a position, including maintaining the status quo, putting the brakes on changes and essentially just ticking over. You will probably not be surprised to learn that this is not what happened at Fortismere in the final year of my headship. We needed to undertake a major restructure that was going to rock the boat in many ways. The restructure was driven in large part by financial pressures, which is never a very appetising reason for change. However, there were many advantages to the changes we had planned, not least new leadership opportunities. A challenge for any organisation where staffing is steady is that you can end up with few opportunities for new leadership at middle and senior levels. In my time at Fortismere, I introduced as many opportunities as I could including new heads of college roles, associate assistant head roles, senior student leadership roles and an array of others. Change is essential to prevent stagnation and complacency but just because it is right doesn't always make it popular and, with the local union always quick to point out the flaws, negatives and imagined agendas, we buckled in for a bumpy ride ahead.

In fact, the restructure went pretty smoothly, and I was ably supported by my deputies who brought valuable perspectives and who had the significant advantage of not having crossed swords with the union rep. By then, I was on a hiding to nothing with that individual and even if I was to offer every member of staff a £500 bonus, my actions would have been misconstrued. Between the three of us, the wider senior team and key governors, the restructure went through its various stages and the key changes were settled, ready for roll-out in September 2017.

The matter of who would lead the school after my departure was a tricky one. My preference was for my deputies to become acting co-heads. This would give the governors time to assess their potential for the substantive headship and would also give more time to recruit from a wider field. I knew I would be leaving the school in very capable hands and could move on in that knowledge. Happily, this plan was agreed and, when I left Fortismere in the summer of 2017, I handed over the reins to my deputies. I am delighted to say that their position as acting co-heads became substantive in 2018 when they were both appointed against a strong field of candidates. This was a very satisfying outcome and I think most heads I know would be delighted to hand on the baton to a member (or members) of their own team.

You're not the head

What does one do after headship? How to avoid the risky scenario of 'those who can, run schools and those who can't, tell others how to run their schools'? I'd had plenty of experiences over the years, both good and bad, of being on the receiving end of well-meant meddling which I had really not appreciated. I had also been led, supported, and guided by inspiring colleagues. I don't believe you can exactly plan to be inspiring as that is very much in the eye of the beholder, but you can at least try to be a help rather than a hindrance and that was what I determined to do in my next role.

In September 2017, I took on my first role at director level as secondary director for The White Horse Federation, a multi-academy trust based in Swindon, with schools in Wiltshire, Oxfordshire, Gloucestershire and Reading. With the exception of two of the secondary schools, most of the schools in the trust served deprived communities. My schools, of which there were seven spanning rural and urban settings, and Ofsted 'good' to 'special measures', included two schools for students with social, emotional and/or mental health (SEMH) issues. Suffice to say, there was plenty to keep me busy!

When working with heads, and goodness knows I knew this having been one for almost twelve years, I knew I had to show that

I had relevant and credible experience if I was going to even attempt to support and challenge them. As the new kid on the block, I wasn't so much concerned about my credibility, as my experiences gained through two successful headships in sharply contrasting schools spoke for themselves. However, I worried about making the shift from leading a school to supporting and guiding others to do so. I wrestled with wondering how much of how I had done things would be relevant and transferable and whether I would know when to push and intervene and when to hold back. Did I get the balance right? Reader, I did not. Well, at least not all the time.

A very dear friend and former colleague once said to me, "Helen, they just weren't ready for your London ways." I smiled ruefully at the time because I knew exactly what he meant, and I also knew the pace I liked to work at categorically wouldn't suit every context or, indeed, colleague. However, I could not slow the pace where significant change was needed for the sake of the safety, welfare and outcomes of students and the words of my most respected and wise chair of governors would come to me in moments of doubt: "Helen, is it right for the children?" Some of my early conversations with new colleagues revealed very wide-ranging appetites for change. Some champed at the bit while others told me that, actually, they were perfectly satisfied with the status quo. Those positions, articulated in that way, were easy enough to work with. It was those colleagues who declared themselves in favour of change and challenge but then defaulted to their former ways as soon as I left the building that were by far the trickiest and most slippery to deal with.

I rolled up my sleeves with great enthusiasm, and set up fortnightly meetings with the seven secondary heads to create a team dynamic and to share the good, the bad and the ugly features of the job in hand. I worked alongside my co-director, who oversaw the primary schools, to create a detailed database of essential information about each school so that progress could be measured and causes for concern flagged up early. I led training sessions on a variety of topics, attended meetings with trustees to account for actions and impact, and tried to get under the skin of each of my schools so that I could better understand their strengths and barriers to progress. This was standard fare for any trust director and was the process I followed in similar roles in three different trusts. What differs from trust to trust, however, is how established tracking systems are, the weighting of vulnerable schools to secure schools and, most critically, how operationally involved the CEO wants to be. The latter really can make or break a trust and the impact and importance of the decisions CEOs make around delegation, autonomy of senior colleagues and transparency, cannot be underestimated.

Education is a small world in many respects and interconnections are almost incestuous. Never assume for one minute that just because you are working in a school in Cornwall that you won't have a link to someone you once taught with in Newcastle. It is just the way we roll in education and is both a blessing and a curse. You will recall how incredibly happy I was at Central despite the significant challenges that popped up every day. You may have wondered what became of it when it closed, merged with another local school and was reborn as an academy. Not to put too fine a point on it, things went horribly wrong and the students and staff from both of the predecessor schools suffered terribly as the academy deteriorated rapidly and lurched in and out of special measures which, for those of you unfamiliar with Ofsted, is pretty much as bad as it gets without being closed on the spot. By a strange twist of fate, this academy had been taken on by the trust and I found myself returning to support it. The day I walked into Gloucester Academy for the first time was both emotional and strange. The building was new, over half the staff were unknown to me, but there were still a number of staff from the Central days. It was my first time to see many of them since 2010 and, suffice to say, it was emotional with a lot of hugs and much catching up about children, grandchildren and other things that life had thrown at us along the way since being disbanded. This reunion was bittersweet as it triggered so many happy memories, but I also felt angry about how Central, once so successful, was now rapidly on the way back down again. Behaviour was appalling with the students using extremely offensive language as normal parlance. In the first four weeks that I worked to support the academy, I was told to "fu*k off" more times than in my entire career to date, and that was just by the staff. I jest! Merriment aside, this was a school in need of rapid improvement and, London ways or not, I was going to have to hit the ground running and take the head with me, *rapidement*!

Responsibility for seven schools, each with its own needs and challenges, was a full-time job and then some. It occupied my every waking hour and, in all honesty, there really weren't enough hours in the day. Add to that a major spanner in the works in the form of jury service. Now, don't get me wrong, I am a big fan of our legal system and having already served as a juror, I knew the importance of the role and the need for all who are called upon to carry out their civic duty. But the timing was lousy, and I really hadn't factored in a second stint of jury service as I was just beginning to settle into my new and demanding role. I did what I could and deferred until March 2018, mindful of the challenges ahead and the fact that my new deputy director was joining the team in January.

March came around all too quickly and one very chilly morning I found myself on the Tube headed for Wood Green. As fate would have it, this was the very day of a fatal stabbing near the Tube station, the first knife-related murder of the year. This was shocking and hammered home what I was about to embark on although, of course, I had no idea what delights awaited me at the court. I vaguely remembered that jury service had involved a lot of sitting around and endless stops and starts as new evidence emerged, witnesses failed to show and so on. I had previously spent ten days in court on two trials and pretty much assumed that this time would be similar.

The initial pool of potential jurors was called into court. I recall there were forty-three of us who would be whittled down based on suitability and availability. The judge was delightful and put us all at our ease while retaining his very significant presence and authority. He explained that the case to be heard was likely to run for six weeks. Gulp! I could feel my heart racing and beads of perspiration beginning to form. This couldn't be happening to me. How the hell was I going to get out of this one? And, if I couldn't get out of it, how the hell was I going to tell my boss that I would effectively be gone for half the term?

We were invited to consider the implications of being away from work and caring responsibilities for six weeks and were allowed to present, in writing to the judge, any mitigating circumstances that we considered made us unable or unsuitable for this term of jury service. I quickly set to work with a summary of my reasons for not being able to serve on this jury. We were each called up to present ourselves to the judge. I will never forget his question to me, "Do all of your schools have their own head teacher?" I confirmed that they did, but explained the vulnerabilities. The judge looked at me not without sympathy but said, "Would any of the schools be unable to function without your presence?" The simple truth was no, and that is what I said. But it made me think about what I was doing and what value I added. This was a thought that came to me often in my time as a director working at various trusts and it nagged away at me.

I was appointed to the jury and spent the next six weeks hearing evidence on a county lines trial. It was tedious at times, depressing, shocking and extremely educational. Having worked with teenagers in challenging settings and with youngsters already steeped in gang culture and operating as links in county line chains, I knew a bit about this world, but this trial was a real eye-opener and my understanding of the grooming process, cuckooing and a variety of other vile practices was greatly enhanced over the six weeks. I will never forget it.

The trial rumbled on into the Easter holidays and those of you who are teachers or in education will know what I mean when I say that losing the whole Easter holiday was traumatic. During my breaks, I tried to catch up on work emails and calls and attempted to maintain a presence at work even though I was up in north London at court. The prospect of more of this grimness continuing throughout the holiday period was, not to put too fine a point on it, crap, but it went with the territory. I was worried about my schools, impending Ofsted inspections, my new deputy settling in and how to maintain relationships with my heads when we had only had six months to get to know each other. There were other significant challenges back at base, so it wasn't as if I could have confidence that the rest of the executive team was there and firing on all cylinders, because it wasn't.

I fretted about Gloucester Academy and had robust meetings with the head. My instincts, trawls through data and days spent on the ground, walking the corridors and dealing with behaviour issues, told me that an Ofsted inspection would result in special measures. I conveyed this to the CEO, the head and other key players. I think it would be fair to say that my assessment was most unwelcome in many quarters, but it was what it was, and I wasn't prepared to say otherwise. With permission from the CEO, I had difficult conversations with the head and team and put in place a rapid improvement plan. At that point, paths diverged and choices were beginning to form. I knew how an Ofsted inspection would go, but that view was not universally shared and, when that happens, nature must just run its course.

The first day after what would have been the Easter holidays but, in my case, was week five of jury service, the expected call from Ofsted came. They'd be in on 17 and 18 April. I picked up the Ofsted message via a voicemail left for me on my mobile phone which was, of course, switched off while I was in court and in the jury room. By the time I knew it was happening, the inspection was already underway. I knew I had to get down to Gloucester for the next day if at all possible, so I arranged to speak with the judge. He very kindly agreed to my absence for one day only and the trial was halted for the following day. As you will understand, a trial cannot continue with a member of the jury missing, so the disruption was huge. My fellow jury members were very decent about this and, considering it would mean the whole jury service extended by another day, they were incredibly stoic.

That evening, after my day in court, I got a train down to Gloucester and was at the academy early the next morning. The CEO and my deputy filled me in on day one. Things were not going well. I was cheered by the news that the lead inspector had recognised my rapid improvement plan and changes to the leadership team as sound decisions and courses of action and, in fact, she said that these steps were a saving grace that showed that the trust was able to take appropriate action. Alas, that wasn't going to be enough to save the academy and, as I predicted, it was judged inadequate and placed in special measures. The team was incredibly sad about this outcome but also energised to press on with the improvements we were beginning to make. I remember those colleagues with great affection and admiration because keeping up one's morale under those circumstances is bloody tough.

With the inspection over, the outcome digested, and some team talks undertaken to make sure we were all clear on the next steps to take in the following week, I was back on a late evening train to London, ready for more jury service the next day. As the train hurtled through the countryside, I found myself longing to stay in Gloucester and the thought of being away from the academy at this point in its journey did not sit well with me.

Over the next week and a half, I tried to concentrate on the trial while diving downstairs whenever possible to check emails and make calls. Added to this new and very real pressure, I had six other schools to worry about and as anyone who has worked in education will tell you, time and schools wait for no man, or woman, and just because Gloucester Academy needed a lot of attention, it didn't mean that the demands from other quarters had lessened. The trial finished and we reached our verdicts on the five defendants. When we filed in that day and the foreman read out our verdicts many of us were in tears at the reactions of the defendants and surprised by how emotionally charged we were. While the crimes committed were dreadful, we had also come to know a lot about each individual defendant over the weeks and, almost without exception, each had a very sad life story.

While I was finishing off my jury service, the CEO decided to pull forward the reorganisation of the trust. I stepped up to become a regional director with Gloucestershire, Oxfordshire and Reading as my patch. I was to take on primary schools as well. It was agreed that I would spend three days a week at Gloucester Academy and do my best to manage the other schools in the two remaining days. This meant spending several nights a week in Gloucester. My youngest daughter was in London taking her GCSEs that summer, so the situation was far from ideal. My husband took over the domestic duties and was there to make sure that home ran smoothly and that my daughter had regular meals and company while I was away. Looking back, it was a big sacrifice to make, and I wish I had put my daughter's needs first. Again, I found myself in a position where personal and professional roles conflicted and, again, I had chosen or been persuaded to choose my professional responsibilities. It seemed there was always a price to pay.

Although I had been involved with Gloucester Academy since September, my touch had been relatively light, as I spent, on average, half a day there per fortnight. The shift to three days per week enabled me to get a head of steam up. Added to that, I was joined in January by my former deputy head from my Central days and it was fantastic to be working together again. It was like the immortal line in *The Blues Brothers* – "We're putting the band back together." It did feel like that and the weeks I spent working with Julian were incredibly happy ones indeed, albeit extremely challenging.

I would like to say that I rode in on my metaphorical steed and cut through the three-headed dragon of bad behaviour, low expectations and hopelessness. But it wasn't quite like that and it required some ar*e kicking, some coaxing and a lot of rolling up of my sleeves and those of close former colleagues who I drafted in to assist with the job in hand. The heat was on and not least because the academy was very much under the spotlight of both the National Schools' Commissioner and our Regional Schools' Commissioner. No pressure then...

Where to begin? Stabilising behaviour was essential and when a block of girls' toilets was set on fire during morning lessons, resulting in the fire brigade and a full school evacuation, it became a pressing matter. Frankly, I had neither the time nor the appetite for trying out experimental approaches to behaviour and decided to bring in BFL, a tried and tested system that my colleagues and I had first learned at Central and that I used at Fortismere. The views of staff and students were gathered in a full review of barriers to teaching and learning. These were then cross referenced and, no surprise, because it always works this way, the barriers identified were the same. This little piece of psychology is essential to the implementation of BFL. It is far harder to disagree with rules when you have all agreed that certain behaviours stop learning, given that schools are meant to be places where you learn and do so uninterrupted. Simples!

A lot of behaviour systems come unstuck early on because of insufficient time given to training staff and students. We spent six weeks working with staff to build the rules and consequences together, practise 'what we would do if...' scenarios and go through the approach to issuing consequences so that students were engaged rather than enraged. Behaviour management is a skill which can be taught. It is the key to happy and productive classrooms and schools. It is not just for Christmas, but is about consistency and day in, day out application and, yes, it can be absolutely tedious. When turning around a school in a pickle you need a combination of quick wins and tangible results that the whole community can see. My colleagues and I decided that the test of the first stage of implementation would be whether we could hold a whole school assembly without total anarchy breaking out. The stakes were high but that gave us the impetus to try even harder. The plan was to hold an assembly after the first full week of BFL in part as a celebration of how far the students and staff had travelled. It could, of course, all go terribly wrong.

After a tough week with inevitable teething troubles, the day of the assembly arrived. Since the day it had opened, the academy had never held a whole school assembly, so this was novel as well as risky. My assessment was that we were ready. I was not expecting our students to have morphed into 'Stepford children' but I knew that the staff now had the tools to anticipate, diffuse and manage poor behaviour. With butterflies in my stomach, I stood at the side of the hall with my assistant director, supporting from the wings. We both knew BFL inside out from our days working together at Central. The head stood at the front of the heart space at the centre of the building, looking ready and, although clearly nervous, emanating excitement. The students filed in silently and sat calmly in their assigned areas. You could have heard a pin drop and the only sounds were of the calming piano music playing for students to enter to and the odd cough or scrape of a chair. I must admit that tears came, and I was incredibly moved by the scene unfolding in front of me. I caught the eye of a number of staff from my old Central days and they winked or nodded by way of acknowledgment that this was what was needed and had been missing. Staff who had worked at the other predecessor school or who had joined the academy in more recent times looked...well, they looked a bit stunned to be honest, as many had voiced the opinion that what we were doing simply wasn't possible with 'these sorts of kids'. If there is one thing guaranteed to get my back up it is phrases such as that and try not to think badly of me, but I must confess, I felt like saying, I told you so. I refrained, of course! With only one exception, and he was dealt with promptly, the students behaved impeccably. It was a wonderful way to start the day and the calm vibe that settled around us all was like balm to the wounds caused by months and years of battling unruly behaviour. Did students continue to behave like this from there on in? Of course not, but what happened that day struck a deep chord and was a shared experience and the much-needed tangible evidence of what was possible with and for our community. It was a shot in the arm that boosted staff confidence. It remains one of my favourite moments in a thirty-year career.

As I mentioned earlier, in April 2018, I was promoted to the role of Trust Regional Director and my patch grew as I took on primary as well as secondary schools across Oxfordshire, Reading and Gloucestershire. As secondary director, I had spent an awful lot of time in bed and breakfast accommodation, on trains and in the backs of cabs. To say it was tiring would be an understatement but the buzz I got from the role compensated for that. I had some tough gigs on my patch and the regional director role did not lessen that, although I no longer had the Swindon SEMH school which was also in special measures. I will always remember my first visit to that school, undertaken with a former Her Majesty's Inspector (HMI) and special school expert. We arrived by cab and walked briskly across the front yard to be greeted by the sight of a little chap up on the roof hurling abuse and bits of glass down at anyone who tried to get in through the front door. His language was colourful and his aim accurate. My colleague and I had to make a run for it to escape being impaled by shards of glass. Fun times ahead, I thought, and I was not wrong. But that is another story that would, by itself, fill a book!

As I hurtled between London, Reading, Gloucestershire and Oxfordshire on various trains, I had time to write up visit notes, plan training, trawl through data and do a variety of other tasks. I also had time to reflect on what I was doing and the difference I was or wasn't making. I felt frustrated by decisions taken to expand our portfolio of schools when the secondary schools were in need of considerable improvement. The trust was and is very effective at turning around failing and vulnerable primary schools but had taken on some really tough secondary schools and, initially, I was pretty much on my own doing that. Seven secondary schools are a big ask and I began to question what I was actually contributing. True, I had bags of headship experience and my colleague heads found it helpful to be able to pick my brains, seek help with bolshie governors and parents and even ask me to step in with challenging students. I was happy to roll my sleeves up and preferred doing that. What I struggled with was asking colleagues to do things I would have balked at when I was a head. At times, I felt like a hypocrite and, me being me, I could not keep my mouth shut and regularly challenged the CEO. Suffice to say, that did not go well and so I moved on from that trust and decided to try my hand at consultancy. I didn't enjoy not being the boss and that was something I had to deal with. I figured that being a consultant would give me more freedom and autonomy, both of which I craved. So, in August 2018, I set up my consultancy company and was then absolutely terrified that I would have no work and no income.

I remain indebted to those individuals who supported my transition from a full-time employed person to a will-I-have-any-work-at-all person. My husband, Mel, was steadfast in his support and encouragement, making what I did possible and successful. Two meetings with two very different CEOs resulted in work that actually began in August 2018 and, in another extraordinary twist of fate, the school that I ended up supporting was Ninestiles. I was delighted to take on this challenge as I had personal and professional ties with Ninestiles and had become firm friends with a number of the Ninestiles colleagues who had supported us so successfully and skilfully from 2006 to 2008. Ninestiles had been an outstanding school for many years and a national leading light. Returning to its once familiar corridors, I was saddened by its evident demise. I remembered visits to the school for training sessions run by Ninestiles colleagues and how inspiring it had been as a place to spend time but now behaviour was poor, teachers seemed either disillusioned or in denial about how bad things had become and it had lost its mojo. Having been rated as outstanding time and time again, the school was in a tricky position that I recognised from my Fortismere days. Maintaining outstanding is really tough.

One of my first jobs at Ninestiles was to get capacity at the senior team end of things sorted swiftly so they could work more efficiently and effectively. The head teacher left at the end of the first week in September, so my original brief to support him had to change. I suggested to the CEO that the two deputies share the role of head and take this on as an acting role with immediate effect. This was agreed upon and we went about making this offer to the deputies. To their credit they accepted without hesitation and so the work began.

Ninestiles is a large comprehensive with 1,500 pupils and over ninety staff. Turning around a ship as large as that was not going to be easy and, as I have already mentioned, doing so against a backdrop of some staff being in denial about the scale of the challenge and the need for improvement made it all the harder. In the early days and weeks, I spent a lot of my time walking the corridors to get a feel for the culture and behaviour and getting to know the staff and students. In the case of the latter, it was sadly inevitable that those I became acquainted with early on tended to be the most challenging.

So, what do you do when tackling a large school in need of rapid improvement? There are many ways to skin a cat, but I didn't have the time or inclination to spend weeks and weeks pondering the various approaches and I relied heavily on previous experience and some gut instinct. To paraphrase a famous quote: good behaviour policies and practices are all alike; every bad behaviour policy and practice is bad in its own way. Now Ninestiles had been a leading light when it came to BFL and many schools around the country, including Central and Fortismere, had been trained and supported by Ninestiles when planning and implementing this policy and approach. But somewhere along the way, Ninestiles had lost the clarity and connection to the simplicity of the BFL philosophy and its message that we are all free to make choices about how we behave but there are consequences associated with those choices. By the time I became reacquainted with Ninestiles, the layers and sub-layers of rules and consequences had become so complicated that it was hardly surprising that staff and students were confused. In addition, newer staff who had joined the school in the last five years had not received BFL training, so what had been a clear and understood system for the more long-standing members of staff, was not so for the newer members of the team, so confusion was magnified and one thing students can sniff out a mile off and fully exploit is confusion, and exploit it they did!

I won't bore you with the detail of the approaches I took but, suffice to say, behaviour leadership was a critical decision and making sure it was in the right hands was of paramount importance. We set about paring the behaviour policy back to core messages, rules and consequences, we ensured that key routines such as whole school detentions were reinstated and we trained staff over a series of sessions through scenarios and modelling what giving a consequence should ideally look like, how to line a class up efficiently and routines around the beginning and end of lessons. Written down, this may look ridiculously obvious but, in fact, it is extremely easy to take things for granted as known and understood and I made many mistakes in the early months around just that. I was guilty of assuming that the collective memory of outstanding behaviour which I had observed during my many visits to Ninestiles back in 2006 to 2008 was secure when, in fact, for the reasons outlined, this was not the case. I had also forgotten the importance of going through and rehearsing routines with staff. If I had my time again, I would have instigated that from week one, but we got there in the end.

One thing I had learned from my own early days of headship and from supporting other heads was the importance of assigning leadership responsibility to individuals and supporting them effectively while also holding them to account. Each member of the senior leadership team had a portfolio of responsibilities which fed directly into the school improvement plan, and it became something of a mantra that 'if it ain't in the plan, we ain't doing it!' Of course, you must develop capacity to respond to unexpected events, but you must also bring the focus back to the key strategic steps to be taken to bring about improvement. I wrote the school improvement plan around key improvement indicators in all areas and each of these had either a numerical or a measurable qualitative target. The team and I met every morning to discuss the operational aspects of delivering the plan and likely hurdles for the day ahead. We also met twice weekly to review progress against the key indicators. Simples! No, not simples!

I have encountered school improvement plans that make the Domesday Book look succinct and I have wondered how anybody could be expected to follow what was supposed to be happening in those plans. I have also worked in schools (in fact, most schools are guilty of this) where students are unaware of the improvement plan even though they are both critical to its success and, arguably, the key stakeholders. My approach to plans was rather different. I used two different approaches over the years and, in both cases, the emphasis was on tangible improvement that the whole school community could relate to and understand. With the balanced score card approach, the whole plan was condensed onto a one-sided document. I still laugh when I remember the faces of some of my governors at Fortismere when I introduced this to them in 2010. "But where is the rest of the plan, Helen?" asked one governor. I could see others nodding. I explained as patiently as I could that this was the plan and that they would be able to hold me to account for the delivery of the key indicators of success. These included hard targets around attendance and performance at GCSE and A level. To their credit, the governors went with the flow and quickly came round to the approach which they found easy to follow and even easier to hold me to account for, which naturally they liked very much!

The other method I used was 'the 100-day plan' which I had learned from my previous CEO at The White Horse Federation. There it had been used to good effect, among other things, to inject urgency into the run-up to GCSEs. I took this model and used it as a basis for half termly improvement cycles which created focus, pace, and rigour through the sheer intensity of activity around key milestones for improvement. Senior colleagues grew accustomed to giving account of their impact over the course of each week and were expected to support their accounts with data. Where progress was not being made it was the team's collective responsibility to suggest ways to get things moving and to lend their support to this. We moved away from individuals working in silos to teams working together with individual lines of responsibility but always with the whole plan in their sights. This shift in work practice took time but I was incredibly proud of the way the team made that shift over the weeks and months and their efforts most definitely paid off when Ofsted came a-calling in December 2019 and Ninestiles was graded 'good'. That was a phenomenal achievement as, in September 2018, it was teetering between 'requires improvement' and 'inadequate'. I had a lot of fun at Ninestiles, and I loved my time there. It reminded me of my happiest days at Central and provided the same range of sublime to ridiculous moments over the course of a day that characterised my first headship. On the strength of that year, I was asked to apply for one of the newly created posts of education director. I was concerned about shifting into being permanently employed again in a role in which I would not be making the critical decisions. I wondered if accepting the post was the right thing to do. Added to that, the commute from London to Birmingham was a killer. But I pushed aside my concerns, applied for the role, and accepted it when it was offered.

Much of the work I undertook for Summit Learning Trust, a multi-academy trust in Birmingham, was similar to that done at White Horse and many of the challenges were familiar. I enjoyed the variety and met some fabulous colleagues, but the commute was hideous, and, by Christmas, I was exhausted and regretting my decision. In addition, I seemed to spend so many hours each week in meetings and I was never good at those unless, of course, I was the one running the meeting. That is just the way I'm built. I had been in charge for twelve years and it was hard to step back. I began to explore opportunities closer to home and, in April 2020, I became education director for Castle School Education Trust (CSET), a trust based in south Gloucestershire which, from a geographical point of view, suited me better. But I was primarily drawn to it because it had a very different catchment and had been the subject of the BBC Two documentary, *School*, which explored the impact of funding cuts. There were clearly interesting challenges ahead.

Lockdown leadership

I assumed my post on 1 April 2020, just as we went into full lockdown. It was an interesting time to start a new role. In fact, it was a bloody ridiculous time to start a new role and I soon found myself in the mad position of trying to support and challenge colleagues via endless Microsoft Teams video conference calls. Trying to establish meaningful working relationships with seven heads, four secondary schools and three primary schools, when I had only visited two of the schools and met each of the heads once on the interview panel, was extremely hard for all concerned. I will try to describe some of the challenges as they presented themselves.

When establishing a team, I wanted the heads to see themselves as part of the wider leadership of the trust, and I needed to find ways to make people feel comfortable sharing their concerns and issues as well as what seemed to be progressing well. My initial impressions were that among the primary heads there was already a well-established collaborative approach to working together. They happily shared ideas about the curriculum, resources for teachers to use and a variety of other documents, including letters to parents and carers. They were quite different in their styles and each school had a unique ethos, but they had reached a sweet spot where they were open, generous with their time and unwavering in their support for each other. In short, they were a pleasure to work with and their approach to working together made those early weeks and months in lockdown less isolating and painful than they might otherwise have been.

As a former secondary head, I know how competitive colleagues can be and I was no exception to that, but I did have a preference for collaboration which was undoubtedly a result of cutting my headship teeth in a federation run on the principle of collaboration through shared accountability. To me, it was both pragmatic and beneficial to seek advice and support from colleague heads and, of course, to reciprocate when I could. However, it is not an easy balance to strike when competition for resources and pupil numbers are clouds hanging in the air. You can't ignore those elements and to imagine that heads would do so would be naive. My experience working with the secondary heads was far more complex and it was predicated on the aforementioned factors. Group discussions were often more guarded and the pattern was that they'd agree a way forward as a group and then call me individually asking whether they could default to the preferred approach. At times, it was like walking through a minefield with politics and history at play that I was only just learning because of the limited ways I could interact with the heads. Body language when interacting on video calls is quite different to that encountered in person and, while many of my initial impressions of individuals proved to be accurate over time, it took far longer to establish trust and work effectively.

I introduced a five-point agenda for each meeting – reputation (teaching and learning), inclusion (attendance and behaviour), standards (outcomes/attainment), every child progressing (progress) and structures (learning environment and staffing). I had used this format at Central, Fortismere and with heads at White Horse and CSET and found it a helpful way of keeping discussions focused on impact and exploring ways to remove barriers to impact. Covid was arguably the biggest barrier, and it wreaked its own particular havoc in many ways, but perhaps one of the most distressing ways was in relation to the most vulnerable students who already had established patterns of poor attendance. The call to stay at home may well have been initially greeted with elation by some students who preferred the safety and peace of their bedrooms but, as weeks turned into months, we heard increasingly distressing news about the impact on those youngsters that schools were already concerned about, as they had started to fall through the gaps. In the case of some schools already working with vulnerable communities, safeguarding concerns grew by the day and staff who had key responsibilities for following these up were, not to put too fine a point on it, on duty pretty much twenty-four seven. I took calls from the heads at all times of the day and evening. They wanted to talk through various cases and steps to be taken. Often there was little I could add as I didn't know the schools, the communities or, of course, the children, but I did my best to make suggestions where I could, to listen carefully and reassure individuals that they were doing the best they could under the circumstances. When students went missing it was always such a joy to learn that they had been found safe and sound. The parable of the lost sheep often came to mind during those discussions and anxious hours.

Full lockdown placed very different pressures on the schools. The teachers, often homeschooling their own children, were stretched beyond breaking point at times. They were nothing short of heroic in how they managed those dual pressures. I came to virtually know people's partners, children and pets as they appeared during meetings. While unconventional, I rather liked those moments of domesticity. They helped to compensate in part for the lack of face-to-face interaction. We laughed about wearing shorts or pyjama bottoms underneath our desks and tables and how the commute from bed to 'office' was only a minute now instead of fifty.

Yes, there were some positive points about lockdown and our ways of working may never be the same again. I remember feeling cheered when I saw families walking past our front gate every lunchtime. Our spaniels loved having both of us around all the time and are definitely less impressed now that lockdown has ended, and they have to spend at least part of the day left to their own devices once again. Relationships bloomed or struggled, family ties strengthened or snapped under the strain, and we all learned a lot about our own tolerance for limited social interaction. A foray to the supermarket for essentials became both a risky business and a thrill. We savoured the daily exercise trip outside, and enjoyed and appreciated texts and calls as never before. I took up letter writing and sent cards to friends and family members which I know they enjoyed receiving. We rediscovered lost arts and simple pleasures which helped us through the hard months. But it wasn't enough to keep everyone afloat.

When the time came to begin planning for the phased return of students, I was struck by how little resemblance my role in these times bore to what I had applied to do or, indeed, to what I thought I would be doing. I spent hours and hours reading, digesting and applying the raft of advice and guidance from the Department for Education. Slight changes made to these hefty documents (often in excess of sixty pages) had to be noted. This often required reading re-released documents that were essentially identical to earlier editions except for a few words or a sentence here or there. My colleagues and I would then try to make sense of our respective sections of these documents and summarise them for the heads to save them the task of trawling through this ridiculous amount of bureaucracy. Don't misunderstand me when I say this, as I was acutely aware of the serious nature of the pandemic and the implications for peoples' lives as we planned for our schools to reopen but, at times, we all felt as if we were on the receiving end of advice that was, not to put too fine a point on it, bleeding obvious and patronising. Perhaps you will think me wrong for saying this, but it was also mind-crushingly boring and the hours spent staring at documents and then regurgitating them into marginally more digestible chunks were easily the most soul-destroying hours I spent during my entire career in education. I dreaded opening the links to those documents, loathed the time spent on bureaucracy no matter how important and missed human contact and the physicality of being in schools. I was not alone in that, but there were, of course, colleagues who seemed to relish that side of things and I say, thank God for them. However, I am not one of them.

It is true to say that I knew more about hand sanitiser, handwashing stations, bubbles and the relative risks of choral singing as opposed to silent music lessons after a few days into the planning than I ever thought possible or indeed wanted to know. I found myself in earnest discussion about the merits of different sanitiser types, how much would be needed, whether our littlest ones would be at risk if they tried to eat or drink it and other dangers lurking in the vicinity of bottles of this stuff. I could hold my own in these discussions, feign interest even, but inside I was screaming. What was I doing? What was the actual point of decades of time spent in schools if it was reduced to such discussions? Of course, we planned for revised curriculums, innovative ways to share resources, how to overcome the challenges for families with no internet provision and many other important educational considerations, but we were all ground down by the health and safety requirements and it made it incredibly hard to maintain any excitement for the academic year ahead with the spectre of Covid looming over us. Excitement and hope are essential, and both were in short supply.

Bursting bubbles

The new academic year began, and schools reopened their doors. Staff and students were generally very pleased to be reunited but I won't pretend that everyone was thrilled to be back because that simply wasn't true. There were staff who were fearful about returning and, in some cases, point blank refused to do so. There were students who had felt far happier at home and simply didn't want to return and that required a lot of patience, reassurance and tenacity to deal with. In some cases, the much hoped for return to school didn't happen despite everyone's best efforts, and I imagine this was the case up and down the country. There was a lot of talk about 'the new normal' but I, for one, soon tired of that phrase as what we were dealing with bore no relation to any kind of 'normal', new or otherwise, and, furthermore, none of us wanted this to be our 'normal' as it was rubbish.

The bursting of bubbles became a daily event. Sometimes several year groups in one school were sent home following tracing of staff and students in close proximity that resulted in a picture of multiple and wide-reaching interactions. There was a sort of novelty factor the first few times this happened and some students saw it as a bit of a laugh. But when this regime of having to isolate at home really began to bite, there were tears of frustration and scenes of real distress which were extremely hard to deal with for all concerned. The disruption to teaching and learning, pastoral support, social interaction, and many other essentials of school life were taking their toll on everyone. Some students responded by becoming withdrawn and depressed, feeling that the whole situation was so out of their control that there was no point even trying any more. Others became angry and manifested behaviour that was extremely challenging at times. Of course, there were also those who managed a stoicism and focus that was remarkable, who kept going as best they could, taking one day at a time. It was humbling to observe students who had this understanding and mastery at such a young age.

What I liked about the reopening phase was that I could actually roll my sleeves up once again and get out and about among the students. I missed the hurly-burly of break and lunchtimes, the strange antics that come to pass in schools on any given day and, of course, I simply missed being around kids, big or small. I opted to help out with duties at one of the secondary schools I was supporting and spent time walking the corridors, chivvying lunch queues, and trying to keep a couple of steps ahead of the game when it came to 'bubble jumping'. As you will know from either your own experience of being a teenager or from observing them, they are adept at finding their way around new systems with the end game in mind of breaking those systems if possible. An example of this was the game of cat and mouse that emerged as students did their utmost to break out of their year group bubbles during break and lunchtimes to cross over into forbidden bubbles. We saw this one coming and schools came up with ingenious ways of keeping year groups separate. It had to be done to maximise the safety of all and minimise the disruption caused when positive cases emerged. The students were well aware of the reasons behind the bubbles and knew the seriousness of breaking out of their bubbles but, try as we might, we couldn't prevent the odd breakaway bubble burster, and break and lunchtimes required us to be hyper-alert to these bubble warriors!

In one of the schools, it had been decided that the new Year Sevens would be located at the front of the school for their breaks and lunchtimes. The logic was that as they were new and most likely to be rule-abiding, this space, which was visible to the general public, was the best one for them and the least likely to result in any incidents that would draw unfortunate attention to the school and damage its reputation. There was a sound logic to this. However, we overlooked the fact that these Year Sevens had not had the usual year of preparation for secondary school transition prior to their arrival and, most significantly, being away from their older peers meant they were not subject to the usual squashing of bumptiousness that usually occurs in September when Year Sevens realise they are the smallest fish in the pond. These Year Sevens arrived in September having had an awful lot of freedom, very little in the way of structure and no sense of themselves as being at the lowest end of the pecking order. The results were interesting.

There were some beautiful trees in a nicely landscaped area at the front of the school. It was a lovely place for the Year Sevens to be gently inducted into the world of secondary education. They listened very nicely to the head teacher's welcome speech on the first morning's assembly and I felt a tear forming as I saw their shining faces looking up earnestly at her and seemingly hanging on her every word as she set out the key attributes that the school wished to develop in its students. With assembly over, they were off to lessons. It was then that we realised that this Year Seven group was not quite what we had anticipated. Now, don't get me wrong, staff at the school understood they were looking at challenges ahead because that was a feature of the catchment, but they hadn't fully factored in how much Year Seven cohorts might vary. They were about to find out!

The newest recruits shuffled out of the hall and were soon on their way to lessons. However, where you would usually expect the odd individual straggling behind the others, later to be found roaming the corridors hopelessly lost, this lot shot out of the hall, gambolling like puppies, with not a shred of concern on their faces and proceeded to scamper down the corridors, leaping like lambs to see if they could 'high five' the ceiling. If they felt daunted by being the new kids on the block, they showed not a jot of it. Getting them all from hall to classrooms was like herding cats and several were super cheeky too. Now, as you know, I have dealt with my fair share of naughties and livelies over the years, been 'effed and jeffed' at on many occasions and encountered bold youngsters, but this lot were off the scale.

Breaktime came, the school was in one piece, and it was time for everyone to let off some steam, while sticking strictly to their own bubbles. At the back of the school, staff firmly but calmly dealt with bubble warriors and applied sanctions when warranted but, at the front of the school…well…frankly, words almost fail me, but I'll try to describe the scene. In the Bible, the Garden of Eden was created for Adam and Eve and their every need is catered to. So it was for the Year Sevens with their lovely landscaped space where they could play to their hearts' content. What did these little souls do to their Paradise? They kick-boxed their way through it, punched, kicked, swore and ripped thin branches from the trees. From my office, I saw this scene unfolding in front of my eyes and was out of the door and running to where the worst behaviour was being enacted. The shocking thing wasn't so much what the students were doing but what the staff on duty were not doing. I was amazed to see two adults standing by while Rome burned, and I spoke pretty sharply to them about their dereliction of duty. Whether they felt intimidated by the students, couldn't be bothered or somehow hadn't seen what was going on in front of them I will never know, but I am glad to say that with my arrival, they bucked up their ideas and we soon had the worst offenders rounded up and spoken to about their behaviour, the school's expectations and what they could and couldn't do. They were quiet and appeared to listen to what we said, but I had a niggling feeling in my mind as I went back to my office that something wasn't quite right. Something told me they weren't really bothered about being in trouble. Call it instinct, but I sensed this wasn't going to be the end of the matter.

Sure enough, within ten minutes, the same students were again ripping twigs off the trees and appeared intent on a duel. Once again, I leaped from my chair and headed out. I was annoyed now and not just with the students. I instructed the staff on duty to fetch the students again and keep them with them until the end of the break. I asked them to issue each student with a detention under the school's behaviour system and to contact the tutors of each student, so that they were aware of what had happened. This was important. It was day one in the school year, so it was essential that the tutors kept a close eye on any behaviour patterns emerging and that they communicated this to other staff, so that there was collective knowledge and understanding, including any specific needs that these youngsters might have. It was not rocket science, but none of these follow-up practices had occurred to the staff concerned. Given that they were both experienced teachers, this was unimpressive, to put it mildly. What this incident revealed was a wider problem concerning staff passivity when it came to dealing with poor behaviour and I saw many more such examples in the weeks and months ahead.

The garden-bashing was a bad start to the term and provided a bit of a shake-up among senior staff who recognised the need to impress upon staff the importance of not just turning up to duty but being proactively involved in it. That didn't go down well in certain quarters, but it needed tackling and everyone's well-being was at stake if behaviour wasn't made a priority. The school settled into the new term and while we lurched from one bubble-bursting incident to the next, staff soldiered on and so did the students. Year Seven continued to be challenging and we discussed whether relocating them to somewhere at least within visual proximity of an older year group might be sensible. The problem was that behaviour was also fairly hairy in all of the other year groups, so we were reluctant to put any of the other cohorts out at the front of the school for the world to see. As is so often the case, events overtook us...

Now, there are things that happen that are just unfortunate, a bit of bad luck or inconvenient, but what happened next with Year Seven was all three rolled up into a big messy ball. As a school, you are constantly managing the ebbs and flows of student and staff interactions and the most successful schools make this look effortless, but the analogy of the swan is never truer than when applied to schools, as it truly is the case that what looks like effortless gliding requires strenuous paddling beneath the surface. The year group bubbles were working pretty well, and it had been decided to keep them where they were but to review the situation towards October half term. Duty staff were reminded to keep year groups separate and those on duty with Year Seven were asked to be vigilant at all times, particularly in relation to certain individuals who had emerged on day one. The Garden of Eden, aka the front of the school, was relatively tranquil and the trees had managed to hang on to most of their branches. We were content. You can, therefore, imagine our horror when a message arrived from a concerned passer-by who had from the road witnessed a young lad in Year Seven being 'bundled' by a group of his peers who then sat on him. The child had appeared distressed, the passer-by saw no adults in the vicinity to alert to this situation, and so he did what anyone would do. He contacted Ofsted. Er no, that isn't what anyone would normally do, but it was too late, and the deed was done. It is fair to say that the gods were not smiling on us that day as our friendly passer-by just so happened to be a HMI, one of Her Majesty's Inspectors and pretty much God in our world. You will appreciate that when we learned of the occupation of our passer-by, we were not at all happy. In education, as in all other areas of public service, one has to develop a certain gallows humour to stay sane and, while there was nothing funny about the incident or the fact that it was witnessed by a HMI, I did have a slightly manic chuckle that evening as I drove home and thought of the famous line, "Of all the gin joints...", but in the context of a HMI who just happened to walk past at that very moment. Hey ho, such is life. There is a happy ending though, as the student was none the worse for his bundling, the youngsters involved were properly remorseful and dealt with robustly and there was no follow-up action from the HMI's contact with Ofsted.

The littlest bubbles

I really enjoyed my visits to the primary schools I worked with and found them refreshing. There is a world of difference between primary and secondary schools and while I had spent my entire career in the secondary sector, I was very aware of the particular charms of the primary sector and the little ones that inhabited it. I adored the tiny chairs, tables and toilets. Yes, even the toilets are cute in primary schools! I loved the displays that filled the walls and hung from the ceilings, the little hands that pulled gently but determinedly at your arms to gain your attention so that you might be shown a drawing, an elaborate mud pie or hear a poem in mid-construction. The openness, the enthusiasm and lack of self-consciousness that typifies many in this age group is beguiling and I would reflect on how and why so much of that is lost during the secondary years. True puberty brings changes that are inevitable, but I remain unconvinced that adolescence is solely to blame, and I think the joylessness that creeps in for the older years stems from the system we have created in this country. As a teenager myself, I found the heaviness of it oppressive and can only hope that I didn't simply replicate that gloom for those in my schools.

Sigmoid curve

Knowing when to move on and make that change is an art and not one I have ever perfected. But over the years, I have had the sense to listen to my instincts more often than not. By November 2020, I realised that I was really not enjoying this role at all. I liked my colleagues and had met some really engaging students, but I felt hemmed in by the bureaucracy, I was not in alignment with some of the approaches to school improvement and I found myself feeling detached and adrift. It was time to make the biggest change of my career to date. It was time to say goodbye to the profession I had joined in 1990. In January 2021, I ended my career and said farewell to a profession that had been a huge part of my life and identity for over thirty years. Walking away felt like free falling off a cliff. It also felt right. Walking away has led to unexpected challenges.

As I look back, my memories flood in and I think again of Ursula and her question to me back in 1989, "Do you always talk out of your fu**ing ar*e?"

Well, Ursula, I'll leave that with you to decide.

Acknowledgements

Huge thanks to all at SilverWood Books for their advice, guidance and expertise. My warmest love and appreciation go to my mum and late dad for giving me such a rich and creative upbringing. Thank you to my little bro for your love and support over the years. To my daughters Dina and Leah I owe a great deal as they travelled some of the toughest parts of this journey with me. My husband Mel has offered unwavering love, encouragement and support, and I thank him so much for this and for keeping me smiling albeit sometimes through gritted teeth.

My dear friends Amanda Butler and Sally Smith have encouraged me when I doubted myself and I will never forget their steadfast friendship. I would also like to pay tribute to my dear friend and former colleague Vanessa Aris M.B.E. without whose patience and support I could never have got through the toughest times. I also owe a great debt of gratitude to Sir Dexter Hutt who introduced me to the wonders of Headship and the Sigmoid curve! Behind every good Head there stand even better deputies and I was blessed with mine.

In particular, I would like to express my great appreciation and affection for my deputies Julian Morgan and the late Martin Shonk. Last but by no means least, thank you to former staff and students across the many schools I attended, taught at or led, accidentally or otherwise!